FABRIC PAINTING
A Simple Approach

Ginny Eckley

Martingale
& C O M P A N Y

x

BOTHELL, WASHINGTON

Credits

President . . . . Nancy J. Martin
CEO/Publisher . . . . Daniel J. Martin
Associate Publisher . . . . Jane Hamada
Editorial Director . . . . Mary V. Green
Technical Editor . . . . Dawn Anderson
Copy Editor . . . . Liz McGehee
Illustrator . . . . Laurel Strand
Photographer . . . . Brent Kane
Cover Designer . . . . Trina Stahl
Text Designer . . . . Stan Green

Fabric Painting: A Simple Approach
© 2000 by Ginny Eckley

Martingale & Company
PO Box 118
Bothell, WA 98041-0118 USA
www.patchwork.com

Printed in Hong Kong

05 04 03 02 01 00   7 6 5 4 3 2 1

FIBER
STUDIO
PRESS

Fiber Studio Press is an imprint of
Martingale & Company.

Library of Congress Cataloging-in-Publication Data

Eckley, Ginny
     Fabric painting : a simple approach / Ginny Eckley.
       p. cm.
     ISBN 1-56477-295-0
      1. Textile painting. I. Title.

TT851 .E25 2000
746.6—dc21   99-086700

MISSION STATEMENT

We are dedicated to providing quality products and service by working together to inspire creativity and to enrich the lives we touch.

CONTENTS

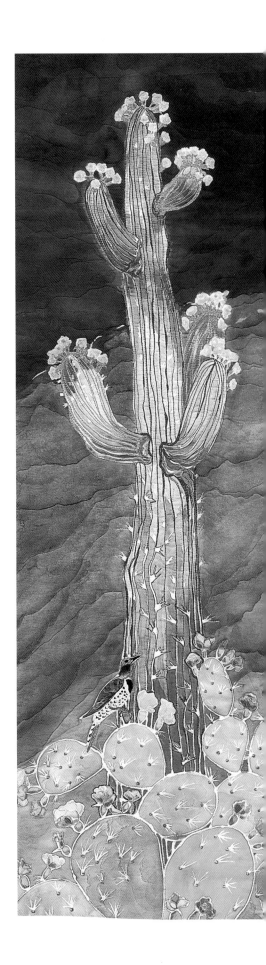

INTRODUCTION

Painting is really an adventure. One idea builds upon another, and before you know it, the creative juices are bubbling. It's an exciting process, one that can change with a stroke of a brush or a dip in a bucket. A big part of learning how to paint is letting go of the end results and experimenting. We are drawn to hand-painted or dyed fabric because of its uniqueness.

It's a thrill as you try new things, realizing in the end that you are better at it than you thought. You did it! All of us have our own style, colors that we love, patterns and subjects that are meaningful to us. We choose the design or concept, add our colors, and in the end, the art fabric is an extension of ourselves. The techniques in this book are easy, attainable, and adjustable to your own individual style.

Isabel's Fantasy Garden II by Joan Toomey

Dyes, paints, and markers

Salt, used with dyes and paints, produces unique effects on a variety of fabrics. See page 15.

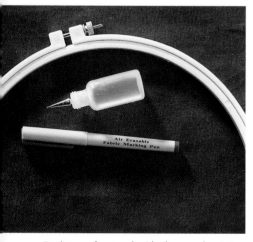

Resist can be used with dyes and paints to produce special effects. See page 13.

Getting Started
Dyes, Paints, and Special Effects

Dyes

Dyes tend to be thin, about the consistency of water. This allows the dye to penetrate through the fabric and bond with the fibers. Some dyes come in a concentrated powder form and need to be mixed with water. The dye I use, Colorhue, comes in a liquid form.

Colorhue Dye

COLORS: Comes in ten colors that can be mixed with one another to create other colors (see "Color Basics" on page 20).

EASE OF USE: The dye is a concentrated liquid and is usually mixed with water. Wear gloves with Colorhue. Otherwise, it will stain your hands for most of the day.

FABRIC: Designed for silk, but also works on wool.

TECHNIQUES: It has the unique property of instantly bonding with the silk fibers. This is the best dye to use for "Painting with Plastics" (page 21) and "Scrunch, Dip, and Dye" techniques (page 23). The colors are extremely vibrant.

CLEANUP: Cleans up easily with water.

FIXING: Allow to dry. Set iron to medium heat; then press on either side of the fabric for twenty seconds.

AVAILABILITY: Can be purchased through Things Japanese.

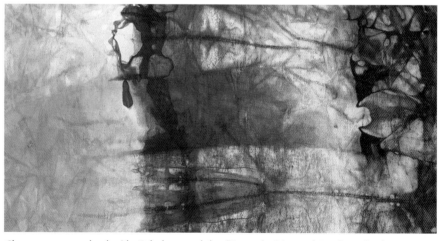

Charmeuse was dyed with Colorhue and the "Scrunch, Dip, and Dye" method on page 23.

Paints

Chances are you already have some fabric paints. Each brand and type of paint has different characteristics. Read the label on your paints for basic information. Often, the better fabric paints leave the fabric softer, and the colors are brighter than cheaper brands. If your favorite paint is not listed, take a scrap of fabric and a paintbrush and test your product. Use the following questions to guide your selection:

- Is the product opaque or transparent? Opaque paints cover and block out the color of the fabric. Transparent colors tend to be lighter, letting the color of the fabric show through. The transparent colors are better for layering color and blending colors together.

- How is your paint thinned or thickened? Paints are often designed for specific techniques. For example, stencil paint is thick, while airbrush paint is thin. Many paints can be thinned with water, while others must be thinned with an extender. Adding water causes some brands of paint to separate, leaving rings that are lighter in color. These paints can be mixed with an extender to thin the paint. You may want to thicken the paint for stenciling. In this case, buy a thickener made by the same company as the paint.

- What types of fabric can you paint on? Some paints are specifically made for natural fabrics, while other paints can be applied to everything from silk to wood. Unlike dye, which penetrates through the fibers, paint lies on the surface, so the texture of the fabric is important. In most cases, a smooth, uniformly woven fabric gives the best results.

- Does the paint need to be fixed or heat set? This is usually listed on the label. Most of the paints I use should be allowed to dry for twenty-four hours and then heat set with an iron. This is important, as most paints have to be set before they are rinsed in water or washed.

Use the paints you have and experiment with the techniques in this book. When you are ready to try a new paint, I recommend the Setacolor transparent paints for the most versatility. The advantage of the transparent paints is that you can paint several colors on top of one another. The fabric will remain soft and the colors are still clear and bright. Following are some of the paints I use frequently.

Jacquard Textile Paint

Colors: Comes in more than sixty great colors, which include metallic, fluorescent, opaque, and transparent.

Ease of use: Jacquard textile paints are thick. To thin, add Jacquard Dye-na-flow.

Fabrics: Works on all fabrics.

Techniques: Use these paints for brush painting, stenciling, sponging, faux batik, and leaf printing.

Cleanup: Cleans up easily with water.

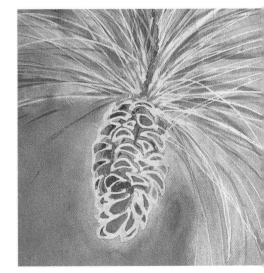

Jacquard textile paint was painted on silk. Resist prevents the paint from spreading into selected areas. See "Resist" on page 13.

Blue-gray-colored tussah silk was stenciled with copper and gold Lumiere.

Blue silk (area below leaping fish) was dyed with Colorhue and painted with white Lumiere.

FIXING: Allow the painted fabric to dry thoroughly. Set the iron to the type of fabric you have dyed; then press on the reverse side for thirty seconds.

AVAILABILITY: Can be purchased through Dharma Trading Company.

Lumiere and Neopaque Fabric Paints

COLORS: The Lumiere paints are metallic, pearlescent, and opaque and are available in sixteen colors. The most popular colors are gold, silver, bronze, copper, and white. The Neopaques are non-metallics, but can be mixed with the Lumiere paints, resulting in colors with a metallic sheen.

EASE OF USE: These paints brush on beautifully. The metallic pigment is heavy and usually separates from its binders. Be careful to stir, not shake, the jars. The paints can be thinned with water or extender. Take care to keep the lids on the paint jars to prevent them from drying out. Metallic Lumiere paints can be used like resist when poured into an applicator bottle (see photo on page 8).

FABRICS: Work on all fabrics, even synthetic blends.

TECHNIQUES: Use these paints for sponging, stenciling, and hand painting. They can be mixed with an extender or with water to create a beautiful metallic wash (see "Metallic Washes" on page 22).

CLEANUP: Clean brushes and stencils with all-purpose cleaner or liquid detergent and water. Do not let your brushes sit in the paint. The paint hardens quickly and will ruin your brushes. I keep a separate set of brushes for the Lumiere, as metallic paint does tend to stiffen the bristles.

FIXING: Allow the paint to dry twenty-four hours. Cover your ironing board with paper towels. Place the fabric on the paper towels, wrong side up, and cover with more paper towels. Set the iron to a cotton setting and press for four to five seconds without moving the iron. If paint comes off on the paper towels, replace with clean paper towels and press again for four to five seconds. Finally, press for twenty seconds, moving the iron.

AVAILABILITY: Can be purchased in a variety of sizes through Dharma Trading Company or Things Japanese.

Novacolor Paint

COLORS: Comes in ninety-six colors, with some unusual metallic colors.

EASE OF USE: This paint goes on like a dream, even the metallics, and leaves the fabric soft when it dries.

FABRICS: Works on all types of fabric.

TECHNIQUES: It is just the right consistency for stenciling. The manufacturer does not recommend adding water because it weakens the binders, so do not use this paint for watercolor techniques or thin washes.

CLEANUP: Clean brushes and stencils with detergent and water.

FIXING: This paint does not require heat setting. Hand wash and line dry. For wearables, allow the painted garment to air-cure five days before laundering.

AVAILABILITY: It is available through Artex.

Mauve-colored tussah silk was stenciled with pearlescent Novacolor. The stencils are by Diane Ericson.

Createx Airbrush Paint

COLORS: Comes in thirty-two transparent colors, twelve opaque colors, and a variety of metallic and fluorescent colors. The colors can be mixed with one another to create any shade you want (see "Color Basics" on page 20).

EASE OF USE: Mix with equal parts of Createx Extender to prevent the airbrush tip from clogging.

FABRICS: Works on all fabrics.

TECHNIQUES: Airbrushing

CLEANUP: Cleans up easily with water.

FIXING: Allow to dry thoroughly. Set the iron to the type of fabric you have painted; cover with a press cloth and press for thirty seconds.

AVAILABILITY: Can be purchased through Bear-Air mail-order company.

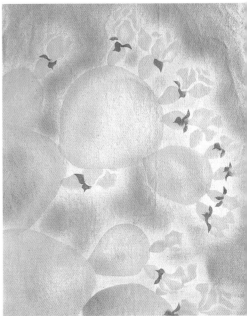

The cactus was airbrushed onto cotton with Createx paint.

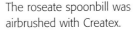

The roseate spoonbill was airbrushed with Createx.

This lotus leaf was airbrushed with Versatex inks.

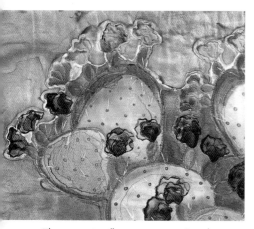

These cactus flowers were painted on silk with Setacolor.

Leaves were placed on silk painted with Setasilk to create this design.

Versatex Airbrush Ink

COLORS: Comes in twenty-five colors and a variety of metallic and fluorescent colors.

EASE OF USE: If using with an airbrush, mix with an equal amount of water to prevent the airbrush tip from clogging.

FABRICS: Works on all fabrics.

TECHNIQUES: Use this ink for airbrushing, hand painting, and stenciling.

CLEANUP: Cleans up easily with water.

FIXING: Allow to dry for twenty-four hours. Set the iron to the type of fabric you have painted; cover with a press cloth and press for thirty seconds.

AVAILABILITY: Can be purchased through Dharma Trading Company.

Setacolor Paint

COLORS: Comes in fifty-eight different colors, including twenty opaque colors, twenty transparent colors, thirteen pearlescent colors, and five fluorescent colors. I prefer the transparent paints, because they allow the fabrics to remain soft, even after multiple layers of paint.

EASE OF USE: Setacolor paint is thick. Use this paint directly from the jar when adding detail; otherwise, thin with water for better paint flow.

FABRICS: Works on all fabrics, even synthetic blends.

TECHNIQUES: Use this paint for sponging, hand painting, faux batik, and sun-printed effects. This paint is a favorite because it is easy to use, the colors are brilliant, and the fabric remains soft.

CLEANUP: Cleans up easily with water.

FIXING: Allow to dry for twenty-four hours. Set the iron to the type of fabric you have painted on, then press on the reverse side of the fabric for two to three minutes, moving the iron as you press the fabric.

AVAILABILITY: Manufactured in France by Pebeo and can be purchased through several mail-order companies. It comes in 45-ml and 250-ml plastic jars and can be purchased individually or in kits.

Setasilk Paint

COLORS: Comes in twenty-nine colors that can be mixed with one another to create other colors (see "Color Basics" on page 20).

EASE OF USE: The paint comes ready to use and is about the same consistency as water. This is an advantage when painting large areas, as the paint spreads more evenly. The 45-ml bottles have a built-in spout, making them easy to use. Dilute the paint with water to create softer shades.

FABRIC: Works on all fabrics. Prewash fabrics to remove any finish.

TECHNIQUES: This wonderful dye has the ability to react with the sun to produce printed images (see "Sun Printing" on page 28). Setasilk also interacts beautifully with salt (see "Salt Effects" on pages 26–27).

CLEANUP: Cleans up easily with water.

FIXING: Allow to dry twenty-four hours. Set the iron to the type of fabric you have dyed, then press on the reverse side for two to three minutes.

AVAILABILITY: Manufactured in France by Pebeo and can be purchased through mail-order companies. The dyes can be purchased individually in 45-ml or 250-ml bottles or in kits.

Fabric Markers

Select markers that are permanent, designed for fabric, and have a firm tip. They can be used on damp fabric to create shading or a soft wash. If you use the markers on dry fabric, you will have sharp lines. You must heat set the fabric with an iron after using markers to make them permanent. Follow the manufacturer's instructions for heat setting.

There are several brands of fabric markers; just make sure that they are labeled permanent. Most have a long tip, pointed at the end. You can hold the marker upright for a fine line, or lay it on its side to create a wider brush stroke. Setacolor markers, called Seta-Skrib+, are great for creating delicate, thin lines. If painted on wet fabric, the lines will spread, blending like paint. If painted on dry fabric, the lines remain crisp. The tip is referred to as a bullet point. The tip remains firm, allowing you to create a thin, long line. They can be purchased individually or in a set of twelve different colors.

The Sakura brush pen has a thinner tip, but it is soft, so the tip bends. Even though the tip looks fine, you cannot create a line as thin as the tip of the pen. They come in eight colors and can be purchased individually or as a set.

Resist

Silkpaint resist is my favorite brand.

COLORS: Comes in clear and black.

EASE OF USE: Mix five parts resist to one part water.

FABRICS: Works on all fabrics.

TECHNIQUES: Paint, sponge, or apply the resist with any tools for an abstract result. Wherever the resist is put on the fabric, the dye or paint will not penetrate. For controlled detail lines, pour the resist into a small applicator bottle with a 5-, 7-, or 9-mm tip. Stretch the silk and draw your design with the bottle of resist. The resist does not have to dry before you apply color.

CLEANUP: Cleans up easily with water.

FIXING: Allow to dry thoroughly. Set the paint or dye first; then remove the resist by soaking the fabric in water for twenty minutes; then rub the resist by hand. Since the resist is detergent based, there is no need to add detergent. Rinse in cool water.

AVAILABILITY: Can be purchased through Dharma Trading Company.

Tip

To keep your pens and markers from drying out, lay them on their sides instead of standing them up.

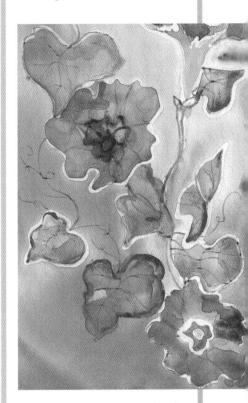

Morning glories were painted with Setacolor. The details were added with markers.

Resist was used with Colorhue on silk to create water patterns.

Salt

Textural effects can be achieved by dropping salt immediately onto painted or dyed fabric. The effects vary, depending on the type of fabric and size of salt used. Additional variations can be achieved by stretching the fabric. The salt technique works with Setasilk or Setacolor. Both Setasilk and Setacolor work on all fabrics, but results are best with silk. Any salt will work, but I like the size of pretzel salt. Other artists I know like rock salt. Salt specifically designed for this technique is manufactured by Deka and sold through Dharma Trading Company.

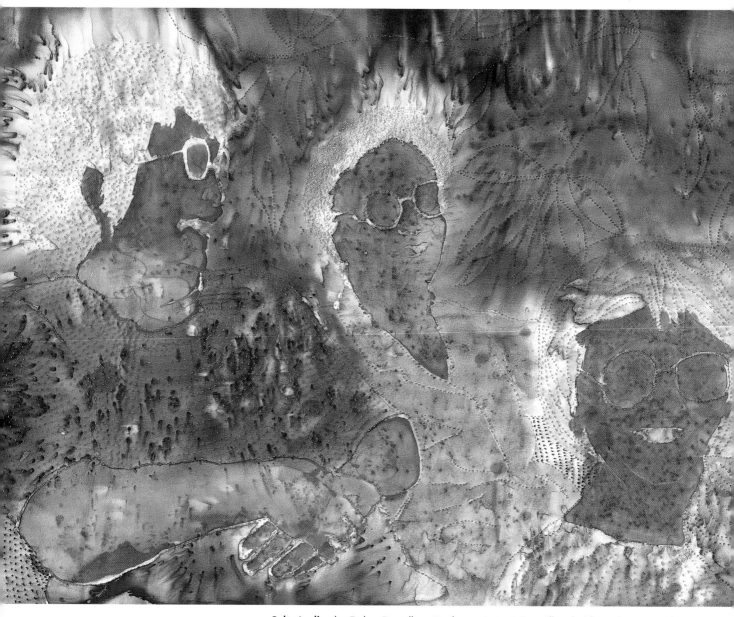

Salty Ladies by Debra Breedlove Puckett, 1999, Gainesville, Florida, 32" x 24". Debra created this beautiful portrait with Setasilk and salt.

China silk with table salt

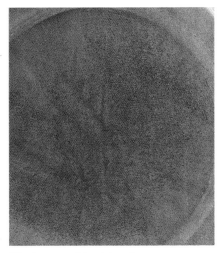

Wool crepe with table salt

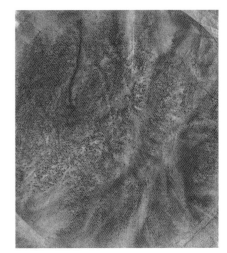

Cotton with table salt

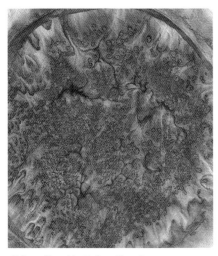

China silk with Deka silk salt

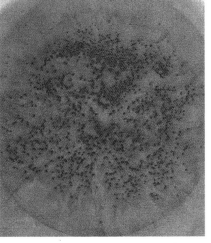

Wool crepe with Deka silk salt

Cotton with Deka silk salt

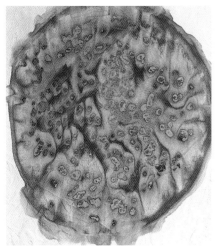

China silk with rock salt

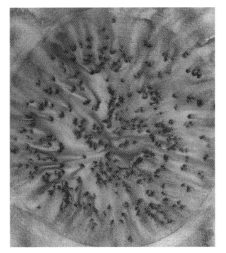

Wool twill with rock salt

Cotton with rock salt

All nine samples were prewashed and dried; then each was placed in a 10" plastic embroidery hoop. The fabric was painted with Setacolor transparent purple, five parts water to one part paint. As soon as the fabric was painted, salt was sprinkled on top. Various effects were achieved, depending on the kind of salt and the type of fabric used.

Tip

Taking Care of Your Brushes

Never allow paint to dry on your brushes. Also avoid letting the brushes sit in water; the bristles will be damaged. After use, wash your brushes in water and a little dishwashing detergent and reshape the tip with your fingers.

Brushes and painting tools

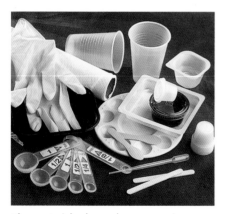

The materials shown here come in handy for mixing and storing paints.

Supplies

Brushes and Painting Tools

Every company has its own name for the same type of brush. Just four inexpensive brushes will get you started. You will probably collect more over time. To begin, choose a ½" flat brush and a 1" flat brush. The bristles are slightly tapered and flat across the tip. They are great for painting sharp edges and blending. Select a script, or liner, brush for thin lines and details. To dampen the fabric before painting, you need a short-hair 3"-wide brush. Disposable foam brushes are also useful. The ones with plastic handles are easier to clean than the ones with wooden handles. Sponges can be used for several purposes. When trying to achieve a mottled look, use a natural sea sponge. For stenciling, I use a dense foam sponge, such as a piece of pillow form.

Materials

In addition to painting tools, you will need a variety of other materials for painting fabric.

APPLICATOR BOTTLES: These ½-oz. plastic bottles can be used to apply lines of paint. They have pointed tips that allow you to create thin, consistent lines. They can also be used to apply resist (see "Resist" on page 13). Metal tips in sizes 5-, 7-, or 9-mm allow you to create lines in three different widths.

CONTAINERS: Start saving plastic containers, especially small ones with lids. These are great for saving paint, and the lids keep the paints from drying out. For quantity, restaurant suppliers sell small condiment cups with lids that are perfect for storing paint. Often, you will mix a special color and will want to save it for design changes or touch-up later. Clear, empty film canisters also work well.

EMBROIDERY HOOP: The hoop stretches the fabric and raises it off the table. Plastic is preferable to wood because wood absorbs paint. Also, wood is not as flexible. The plastic ones are inexpensive and can be purchased at discount stores.

EYE DROPPERS/PIPETTES: These work well for mixing dyes and dropping small amounts of dye directly onto the fabric. I use them for the "Scrunch, Dip, and Dye" method on page 23.

FLEECE: When I am painting large pieces of fabric, I cover a piece of foam board or cardboard with plastic, then tape fleece over that. This sandwich provides a flat, stable surface and allows me to paint large pieces without stretching the fabric. The fleece absorbs the excess paint while the plastic prevents paint from absorbing into the foam board or cardboard.

FOAM BOARD: This is a great product that can be easily cut with an X-Acto knife. It provides stability when you can't use an embroidery hoop. For instance, to paint a jacket sleeve or a pant leg, I have cut long, narrow pieces and slipped them inside. The foam board allows the fabric to lie flat so you can stencil or paint on a smooth surface.

FREEZER PAPER: This product has a waxy side that is a perfect stabilizer for slippery silks. I often use it when stenciling or airbrushing. Simply press the wrong side of the fabric to the waxy side of the paper. The paper comes 18" wide and can be found in the paper-goods aisle of grocery stores.

GLASS: When you cut stencils, the X-Acto blade will cut through the plastic and into whatever is under the plastic. To protect your table, place a piece of ⅛" glass under the plastic before you begin cutting. Cover the sharp edges of the glass with tape. Another option is to use a mat designed specifically for the X-Acto knife. Do not use a rotary-cutter mat, because the X-Acto knife will cut into the surface.

GLOVES: Disposable gloves can be purchased in the pharmacy department. Paint departments also carry them; however, the ones in the pharmacy are hypo-allergenic. They can be purchased in small, medium, or large sizes. I prefer the disposable ones because they are thinner, making them easier to work in.

MIXING STICKS: Often, paint directions will recommend stirring the paint rather than shaking, as shaking creates air bubbles. Popsicle sticks, coffee stirrers, and plastic drink sticks all work fine.

PLASTIC DROP CLOTH: Be sure to cover your work surface when using paints and dyes. A plastic drop cloth from the hardware store works well.

STENCIL BURNER: This optional but handy electric tool makes cutting stencils very fast. The fine tip allows you to create intricate designs.

STENCIL TAPE: This tape will not leave sticky residue on your fabric like masking tape will. Still, do not leave the tape on for long periods of time or in the sun. A similar tape is drafting tape or low-tack tape.

X-ACTO KNIFE: This easy-to-use tool allows you to cut intricate designs from plastic to create stencils. You can also use it to cut foam board. The best blade is the fine point.

Fabrics

DYEING AND PAINTING TECHNIQUES can be used on a variety of fabrics. For best results, prewash your fabrics to remove any finishes. Most of the fabrics I use are purchased through mail-order sources. They are designed for dyeing and painting and do not have finishes on them.

I prefer to start with white silk so I can achieve a full range of colors when I paint. However, you can paint on colored fabrics. The Orchid design in "Hand Painting with Setacolor" on page 30 was painted on colored cottons. If you use transparent paint on colored fabrics, the paint colors will blend with the color of the fabric. If you use opaque paints, the paint will cover the original fabric color. Note that fine details do not print well on open weaves or fabrics with thick threads. Threads with lintlike fibers on the surface are also more difficult to paint on. I do recommend that you hand wash and hang dry painted clothing, as those methods are not as harsh as machine washing or dry cleaning.

Silk Fabrics

My favorite fabric to dye and paint with is silk. No other fabric has the same radiance or so quickly takes the dye. Silk comes in a variety of textures and weights. The weight is measured by *momme* (pronounced "mommy"), a Japanese unit of measure commonly abbreviated as *mm*. The higher the momme, the heavier the fabric. I recommend working with silks that are 18 to 23 mm because they are more stable for painting and sewing.

When ordering silk by mail, request samples of the silks before you place your order. This will give you the opportunity to see and feel the fabric and compare different silks before purchasing. The following are a few of my favorite silks.

CHARMEUSE: This fabric has a smooth satin finish with a rich sheen and a soft crepe back. It is available in weights from 12 to 23 mm and widths up to 55". It drapes beautifully and works well with all the painting and dyeing techniques.

CHINA SILK OR HABUTAI: This silk has a smooth, even weave. It comes in a variety of weights and widths. The heaviest available is 16 mm, which works beautifully for painting and dyeing. *Habutai* means "soft as down" in Japanese.

CREPE DE CHINE: The weft threads are tightly twisted, resulting in the pebbly, uneven texture that makes this

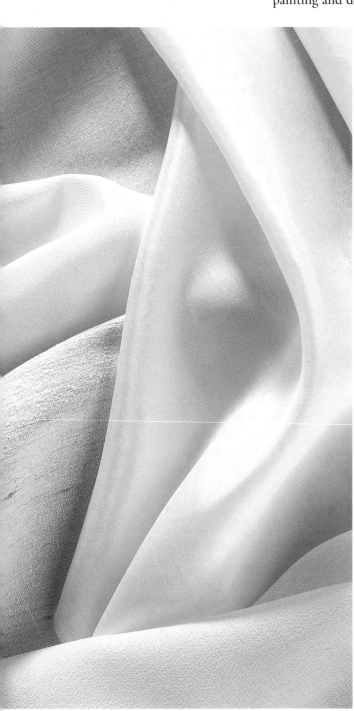

White fabrics for dyeing

fabric unique. It is a terrific texture for creating depth, making it my favorite silk for backgrounds. Since it is not a smooth surface, this fabric is not the best for stenciling or faux batik. It is great for dip-dyeing.

DUPIONI: This is a tightly woven silk, with a crisp drape. It has a beautiful sheen and is textured with irregular slubs. I like it best for overall dyeing and stenciling rather than painting.

RAW SILK OR SILK NOIL: Slubs or nubby spots create the texture in this fabric. It comes in shades from beige to brown, with varying finishes from matte to a soft luster. Due to the slubs, it is best used for overall dyeing rather than painting. Often the slubs show up more after dyeing.

SATIN: This silk is stiffer than charmeuse, but has a similar sheen. It is a great choice for any of the techniques in this book.

TAFFETA: The stiff feel, or hand, distinguishes it from other silks and makes it easy to work with. The most common weight is 13.5 mm.

TUSSAH SILKS: These silks are naturally cream to brown in color and come in a variety of weaves. The silk is spun from oak leaves rather than mulberry. It is available in different weights.

Other Fabrics

COTTON: You can paint on cotton in a variety of weights. I prefer a fine cotton with a 200-thread count. Prewash and dry the fabric to remove any finishes and to allow for shrinkage.

WOOL: This fabric is available in several weights and weaves. A smooth wool can be painted on, while textured weaves are best for dyeing.

SYNTHETICS: I often paint clothing that is a polyester-and-cotton blend, which travels well. I also use polyester fabrics for painted table linens, since they don't have to be pressed.

Work Space

I AM OFTEN ASKED ABOUT MY STUDIO. Over the years, I have had studio space that varied from a kitchen table to a two-story building. I believe you can create and paint wherever you are. I have even done it in my hotel room. What you need is good lighting and a table covered with plastic. If you tend to be messy, cover the floor with a drop cloth and tape it down. Then you need disposable containers, such as plastic cups, coffee stir sticks or Popsicle sticks, and an empty container or bucket to put dirty water in. Having a sink nearby is handy, but an empty container will work just fine. The only common-sense precaution is not to reuse the containers or utensils for anything but paints or dyes.

The products I use are water-soluble and non-toxic. I find gloves difficult to work with when I paint; however, I do recommend using gloves with Colorhue dyes, as they stain your hands.

The one technique that requires health awareness is airbrushing. Do use a face mask, as a lot of paint goes into the air around you. Disposable masks can be purchased in paint departments. If your compressor is loud, use earplugs, or use an extension cord and move the compressor as far away as possible.

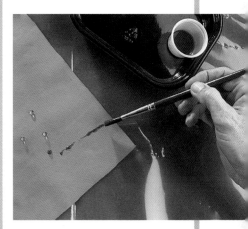

This fabric was treated with finishes. Water and paint bead up, as they are not absorbed into the fabric.

Color Basics

A COLOR WHEEL IS A GOOD REFERENCE TOOL that guides you as you mix dyes and paints to create colors. It can be purchased at art-supply stores and is a timesaving investment. The following are some basic color terms you will find helpful.

PRIMARY COLORS: These are colors that cannot be created by mixing other colors. There are only three primary colors: yellow, blue, and red. These are the basic colors you need to mix all other colors. These three, along with black and white, will allow you to create the full spectrum of colors.

SECONDARY COLORS: Mixing two primary colors creates a secondary color. Red and yellow create orange, yellow and blue create green, and red and blue create purple.

COMPLEMENTARY COLORS: Two colors that are directly opposite one another on the color wheel are complements of each other. In a pair of complementary colors, one is cool and the other is warm. Together, the two colors create a harmony, distinct and striking. An example in nature is a purple pansy with a yellow center. Red and green are complementary colors, as are blue and orange.

TERTIARY COLORS: Mixing one primary and one secondary color together will create a tertiary color. Turquoise is a good example, created by mixing the primary color blue with the secondary color green.

WARM COLORS: Reds, oranges, and yellows

COOL COLORS: Blues, greens, and violets

HUE: Another name for color

INTENSITY: Brightness or dullness of a color

VALUE: Lightness or darkness of a color

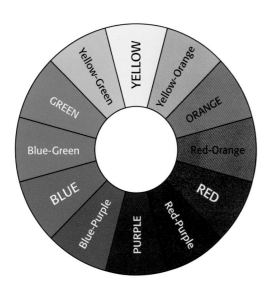

TINT: Adding white to a color creates a tint.

TONE: Adding gray to a color creates a tone.

SHADE: Adding black to a color creates a shade.

Painting Techniques
Painting with Plastics

THIS IS A FAST, EASY WAY to create abstract patterns. Spread out thin dry-cleaning bags or plastic bubble pack on your table; then place fabric on top. Brush the fabric with water and paint with Colorhue. The fabric instantly picks up images from the plastic, creating unique patterns.

Materials

Smooth silk
Colorhue dyes
2"-wide foam brush
Plastic dry-cleaning bag
Disposable gloves
Plastic drop cloth
Masking tape
Iron and ironing board

Fabric Painting on Dry-Cleaning Bags

Directions

1. Cover the table with a plastic drop cloth and tape it in place.
2. Cut the dry-cleaning bag apart at the sides and across the top. If the bag is printed, the inks can transfer to your silk, so use only the unprinted parts of the bag. Take a piece of the bag and lay it on the table, wrinkling it, or for small pieces, place wrinkled plastic inside the lid of a box. The plastic needs to be about twice as large as the size of your fabric.
3. Lay the right side of the silk on top of the plastic and smooth with your hands. Lightly dampen the silk by brushing it with water with the foam brush. This will allow the dye to spread evenly.
4. Put on your gloves. Dilute the Colorhue dye: 2 parts water to 1 part dye.
5. Brush the dye onto the silk; do not move the silk. Let the silk dry on the plastic. Note that the side of the silk touching the plastic will be stronger in color because the dye settles into the wrinkles of the plastic.
6. Allow the fabric to dry for 24 hours. Rinse in cool water and allow to dry. Set the dye by pressing the silk with an iron set on the silk setting. Press for 30 seconds on each side.

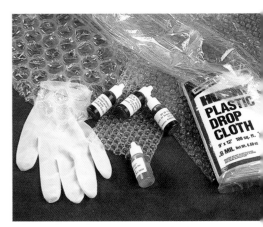

Materials needed for painting with plastics include dry-cleaning bags, bubble pack, Colorhue dye, disposable gloves, and a drop cloth.

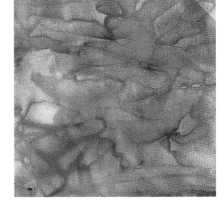

Silk was painted on top of a dry-cleaning bag with blue, green, and black Colorhue dye.

Step 5 of "Fabric Painting on Dry-Cleaning Bags"

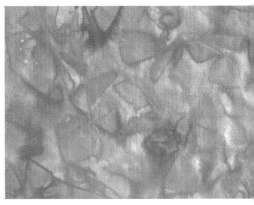

Silk was painted on top of a dry-cleaning bag with green Colorhue dye.

Step 5 of "Fabric Painting on Bubble Pack"

Fabric Painting on Bubble Pack

Follow step 1 on page 21 for "Fabric Painting on Dry-Cleaning Bags." Lay small or large bubble pack over the plastic drop cloth or inside a box lid, textured side up. The bubble pack is not wrinkled, unlike the dry-cleaning bag. Continue as in steps 3–6 on page 21.

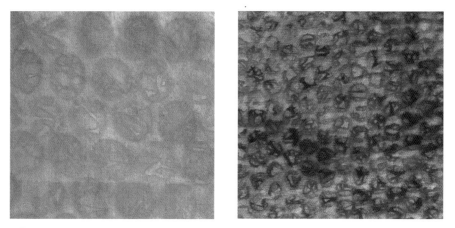

Silk was painted on both large and small bubble pack with turquoise Colorhue.

Tip

For smaller silk pieces, paint on the plastic inside a box lid. This allows you to move the box lid from your table while the silk dries.

Metallic Washes

Use metallic washes to give a sheen or sparkle to your fabric. If doing multiple layers of dyeing and painting, heat set the fabric before applying a metallic wash. There are several brands of metallic paint, but Lumiere is my favorite. Follow the technique for "Fabric Painting on Dry-Cleaning Bags" on page 21 or "Fabric Painting on Bubble Pack" above; then apply a metallic wash over the silk as follows: Start by mixing four parts water to one part metallic paint. Stir the paint mixture and brush over a scrap of silk to test. Add more paint or water for the desired effect. Cover your table with plastic. Place the pressed fabric on the table, right side up. Using a sponge brush, paint the wash over the fabric. Allow to dry twenty-four hours, then heat set, following the Lumiere fixing directions on page 10.

The sample was painted on a dry-cleaning bag with black Colorhue dye, dried and heat set, then painted with a copper Lumiere wash.

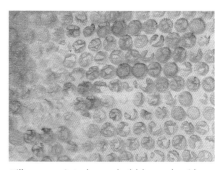

Silk was painted over bubble pack with Colorhue dye, dried and heat set, then painted with a gold Lumiere wash.

Scrunch, Dip, and Dye

This is a fun, easy way to give a tie-dye effect. It works with all types of silk and is great for backgrounds. The key is to wad up the silk and place it in a small container so that the dye is distributed unevenly. With large pieces or yardage, some areas may remain white.

Materials

Silk
Colorhue dyes
Clear plastic cups
Disposable gloves
Plastic drop cloth
Masking tape
Pipette or eye dropper (optional)

Directions

1. Cover the table with a plastic drop cloth and tape the drop cloth in place. Put on your gloves. Mix 3 capfuls of Colorhue dye into 1 cup of water in a plastic cup. Add more dye for a darker shade. Repeat this process to create a second color in a second plastic cup and a third color, if desired.
2. Wad up your silk and place it in the lighter color first. Leave it in the dye for 5 to 10 minutes.
3. Rinse in cool water. Repeat step 2 for the second color. Repeat for a third color, if used. Rinse and hang to dry.

Adding Spots to Scrunch, Dip, and Dye Fabrics

Use a pipette or eye dropper to add spots of color to your dyed fabric. Since Colorhue is concentrated, mix the dye with water before dropping it onto the fabric. Colorhue sets so quickly, the new color will absorb instantly, without changing the colors around it. If you try this with other dyes, the color you get is often brown.

China silk was colored with blue, yellow, and green Colorhue dyes.

Silk taffeta was dyed with pink and turquoise Colorhue dyes.

Dropping color with a pipette

Silk was colored with green, yellow, and pink Colorhue dye. The spotty effect was created by dropping the colors onto the fabric with a pipette.

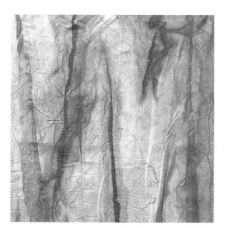

Silk was squirted with purple, black, and copper Setacolor paint and then pleated.

This scarf was painted with gold, red, and purple Setacolor paint and then pleated.

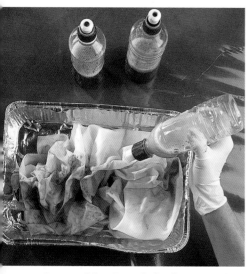

Step 2 of "Squirt and Pleat"

Squirt and Pleat

For the squirt-and-pleat method of painting, diluted paints are put into squirt bottles and squirted onto the fabric. The fabric is then placed over plastic and hand pleated. The surprising effect with Setacolor is that the color wicks to the top of the silk, producing a stronger color along the pleat line. This is a fun and fast way to paint yardage.

Materials

Silk fabric
Setacolor paints
3 water bottles with pop-tops
Aluminum roasting pan
1-cup measuring cup
Plastic drop cloth
Iron and ironing board

Directions

NOTE: I recommend using two colors plus one metallic color. Too many colors make this technique look overdone.

1. Pour 1 cup of water into a bottle; then pour 1 capful of paint into the bottle. Add the pop-top. Make sure the pop-top is pushed down. Shake to mix the paint; mix well so the pigment is dissolved. Repeat for the second color and again for the metallic color.

2. Place the dry fabric into the pan. Squirt on colors. Do not squirt so much that the bottom of the pan fills up with paint. Swish the silk around, soaking up any excess paint. Make sure that all the fabric is dampened by the paint.

3. Lay out the plastic drop cloth on the table or floor. Place the fabric over the plastic. Pleat the fabric by hand, creating ridges. The ridges, or highest part of the fabric, will wick the paint, making the darkest lines on the top of the pleat.

4. Let the silk dry completely. Following the directions for fixing under "Setacolor Paint" on page 12, press to set the paint; then rinse and dry.

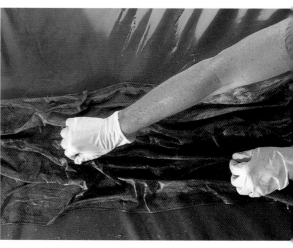

Step 3 of "Squirt and Pleat"

Sponge Painting

Natural sea sponges add a beautiful pattern and texture to fabric. I often paint the fabric a light color first, let it dry until damp, and then sponge on bright colors. This technique works with a variety of paints. I have used this method in my artwork to convey trees and fields of flowers. If you sponge on color while the fabric is damp, the paint will spread, resulting in soft, muted patterns. If you sponge on resist (see "Resist" on page 13) and then sponge on color, you can achieve a bubbly look.

Materials

Fabric
Fabric paints
Sea sponges
Plastic trays (Take-out restaurant containers work great. You can put the sponge on one side and the paint in the other.)
Scrap paper
Plastic drop cloth
Masking tape
Iron and ironing board

Directions

1. Cover the table with a plastic drop cloth and tape it in place. Dampen the sponges in water; then squeeze out excess.
2. Place a spoonful of paint in a plastic tray and dab the sponge into the paint.
3. Always test the sponge painting on paper first. Often a blob of paint may be hidden in one cell of the sponge. Lightly rock the sponge onto the paper. You can usually print with it a few times before dipping it in the paint again.
4. Stabilize the fabric by taping the edges to the plastic drop cloth. Sponge onto dry fabric for crisp shapes. For a softer look, sponge onto slightly damp fabric; the paint spreads, creating a beautiful, muted pattern. If the fabric is too wet, the sponging pattern disappears.
5. Let dry for 24 hours; then heat set by ironing for 2 to 3 minutes.

Several sea sponges, each dipped in different colors of Setacolor, were used to create this mottled effect on silk.

Cotton was painted blue and then sponge painted when it was quite wet.

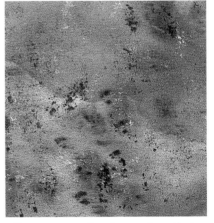

Silk crepe was painted turquoise, dried until damp, sponged with green, dried, and sponged with red, purple, and white.

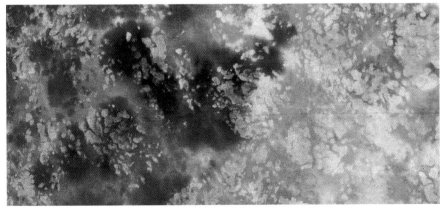

Silk was sponged with resist and then sponged with paint (see "Resist" on page 13).

Salt Effects

NOTE: See "Salt" on pages 14–15.

A variety of results can be achieved with this simple technique. Dropping salt onto painted or dyed fabric draws up the paint or dye, causing the colors to flow in different directions, creating unique patterns.

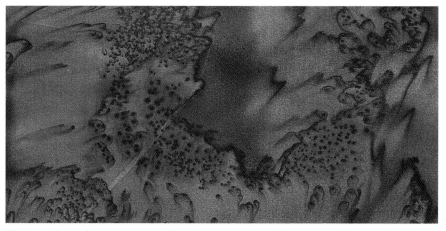

Blue, purple, and turquoise Setasilk and pretzel salt produced these results.

Materials

Prewashed fabric
Setacolor or Setasilk paint
Foam brushes, one for each paint color
Table salt and salt shaker, Delta silk salt, rock salt, or kosher salt
Plastic embroidery hoop or frame to stretch fabric
Iron and ironing board
Plastic drop cloth
Masking tape

Step 2 of "Salt Effects"

Directions

1. Cover the table with a plastic drop cloth and tape the plastic in place. Place the fabric in the embroidery hoop, right side up. Place the hoop with the screw on top, so the fabric is suspended. Stretching the fabric makes the salt pattern more defined.
2. Mix the paint with equal parts water. Work in small areas, so the paint does not dry before the salt is sprinkled on. Paint and immediately sprinkle on salt.
3. Allow to dry in the sun if possible.
4. When dry, brush off salt. Allow to air cure for 24 hours. Heat set by laying muslin over the fabric and pressing it 2 to 3 minutes with an iron. Rinse in cool water to remove salt deposits and let dry. This seems backwards, but if the fabric is rinsed before heat setting, some of the paint will wash out.

Spotted Pattern

Place fabric in the embroidery hoop. Sprinkle on salt first; then paint up to the salt. This allows you to take your time when designing a salt pattern.

Ring Pattern

Start by painting a circle of color; then sprinkle salt around the edge. Paint a second color around the circle, and sprinkle salt around the outside edge. Continue, repeating the pattern. The two colors blend, creating a third color or different shade.

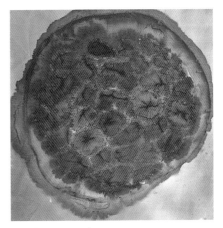

Purple spots, salt pattern

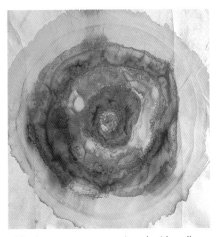

This ring pattern was painted with yellow and blue Setacolor that blended, creating green areas.

In a silk-painting class in Florida, one of my students, Debra Breedlove Puckett, created this beautiful portrait, "Salty Ladies," with Setasilk and salt. (Detail above.) She says, "I drew the original design with resist. Then as I painted each section, I added salt. As the paint was drying, someone accidentally spilled dye on the design, so I sprayed water on it trying to remove the dye. This caused the resist to break down, and my colors moved. The design changed, but what I love is that the motion of the colors mimics the laughter and love between my mother, grandmother, and aunt."

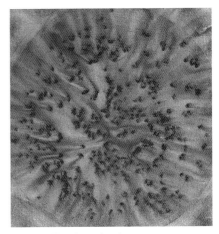

Wool twill with rock salt

Leaves, placed on silk painted with Setacolor, created these images when the fabric was placed in the sun.

Leaves were printed with Setacolor, then the background was painted with Setacolor.

Leaves with prominent veins work best for this technique.

Sun Printing

The Pebeo products Setacolor and Setasilk change values when objects are placed on top of the painted fabric and put in the sun to dry. To produce sun-printed effects, stretch the fabric in a hoop; then brush on Setasilk or Setacolor. Quickly lay flat objects on the surface of the fabric and place the fabric in the sun to develop. Distinct patterns are formed on the fabric as the objects block out some of the color. The key to a crisp design is stretching the fabric taut and choosing flat objects with intricate edges or openings, such as a paper doily.

Leaf Printing

We have all seen leaf prints before, but a few tips can make all the difference in achieving beautiful results. I have been amazed at how many types of leaves will print nicely. I usually print with green paint and add touches of color for interest. The key ingredients to successful prints are choosing leaves with raised veins on the back side, painting evenly, and pressing firmly. A smooth, evenly woven fabric works best with this technique. When collecting leaves, keep 2" to 3" of the stem with the leaf. I cut 12"-long branches, place them in water, and remove the leaves as needed.

Materials
Fabric
Thick, water-based fabric paint (Almost any brand will work.)
½" soft, flat brush
Liner brush
Leaves
Tissue paper
Scrap paper
Resist
Plastic drop cloth
Masking tape

Directions
1. Cover a table with the plastic drop cloth and tape it in place. Lay several sheets of scrap paper on the plastic and place the fabric over them.
2. On another piece of paper, using the ½" flat brush, paint the back of a leaf and the stem.
3. Place the painted side of the leaf down on a piece of scrap paper.

Step 2 of "Leaf Printing"

4. Place tissue paper over the leaf. Press on the tissue paper, being careful not to move the leaf. The tissue absorbs excess paint.

5. Remove the tissue. If the leaf still has some paint on it, you can repeat step 4 to produce a lighter print. Once you have practiced and are happy with your results, repeat the same process on fabric.

6. Use a liner brush and green paint to extend the stem lines or to add definition to the leaves.

7. Paint the area behind the leaves if desired. Before painting, apply resist around the leaves if you are concerned about the paint bleeding into the leaves (see "Resist" on page 13).

Step 4 of "Leaf Printing"

Multiple colors of Jacquard paints were used for this leaf print.

Printed oak leaves create the border on this quilted wall hanging.

Hand Painting with Setacolor

by Joan Toomey

AUTHOR'S NOTE: Joan Toomey is a terrific artist and teacher. For years, she painted with watercolors, and now she has transferred those skills to fabric. She designs and paints beautiful, hand-appliquéd art quilts and clothing. Several years ago, she suggested I try Setacolor paints, and I have been using them ever since. I am thrilled and honored that she agreed to write about this technique. For instruction purposes, an orchid pattern designed for appliqué will be used. The same painting techniques can be applied to other designs of your choice.

Orchid, hand appliquéd
by Joan Toomey

SETACOLOR comes in both transparent and opaque colors. I prefer the transparent paints, as the fabric remains soft even after several layers of paint are applied. Also, the color of the fabric underneath the paint shows through, creating more color blending. To add glimmer to the transparent colors, mix in a small amount of Setacolor metallic paint.

The essence of this technique is that when the fabric is damp, the paint spreads, resulting in soft, muted colors. When the fabric is dry, colors are darker and lines are sharper.

When trying to produce shading, think of where the sun hits the flower or leaf. For example, if the sun is in the upper-right corner, the light will make the colors brighter on the upper-right side of the leaves and petals. Areas farthest away from the sun will be the darkest.

Hand-Painted Orchid

Materials

Cotton fabric in hot pink, bright yellow, medium to light green, and your choice of background fabric (If you plan to hand appliqué the orchid, choose cotton fabrics that are tightly woven with fine threads.)

Setacolor transparent paints in purple, green, yellow, and fuchsia (These color suggestions are guidelines; you can choose your favorite colors.)

Several inexpensive paintbrushes, varying in size from a liner to a 3" brush

14"-square of thin, flat batting to help absorb excess paint

Fabric markers

Chalk pencil

Tracing paper

Container for water

Plastic drop cloth

Masking tape

Paper towels

Iron and ironing board

Directions

1. Trace the pattern pieces for the flower components (page 32) onto tracing paper. Trace the leaf patterns on page 33 and tape them together on the dotted lines. Mark the top just outside the pattern edge. Transfer the pattern pieces onto the corresponding fabrics using a chalk pencil. Leave 1" between the pieces.

2. Write the pattern number next to each piece. The leaf pieces are 1 and 2, and the yellow pieces are 3, 4, 5, and 6. The pink pieces are 7, 8, and 9.

3. Cover your table with plastic; then place the batting on top. Start with the green fabric for the leaves. Place it on top of the batting. Using a large brush, lightly dampen the fabric with water.

4. Dip your ¼" to ½" flat brush in clean water. Lay the bristles of the brush on a paper towel, first one side and then the other. This takes excess water out of your brush. Shake a bottle of Setacolor lightly and open. There will be a little paint in the cap. Now dip your damp brush into the paint in the cap. Starting at the outside edge of the pattern line, drag your brush toward the center. Don't worry if the paint spreads beyond your pattern line.

5. To make the leaf appear dimensional, paint a dark color, such as purple, blue, or a dark green, along the outside edges. Paint yellow on the inside. If you don't like what you just painted, take it immediately to the sink and rinse in soapy, lukewarm water. Most of the color will wash out, and you can repaint the fabric when it is damp.

6. To paint the flower, follow the process in steps 4 and 5. Use small brushes and purple and fuchsia paint. Paint darker tones along the edges and just vein lines in the center. Add accent lines with markers.

7. Add vein lines to the leaves with marking pens, or paint them in with a liner brush once the fabric is dry. Heat set the paint as directed on page 12.

8. Following the method for either hand or machine appliqué as on pages 47–49, appliqué the orchid pieces to the background fabric.

Tip

Don't tighten the caps of the Setacolor jars too tightly. The cap will crack, causing the paint to dry out.

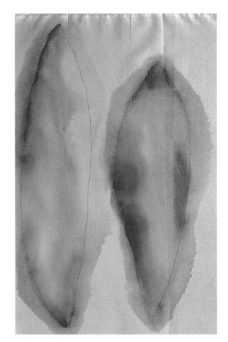

Painted leaves

Yellow sepals, accented with markers and Setacolor transparent paints

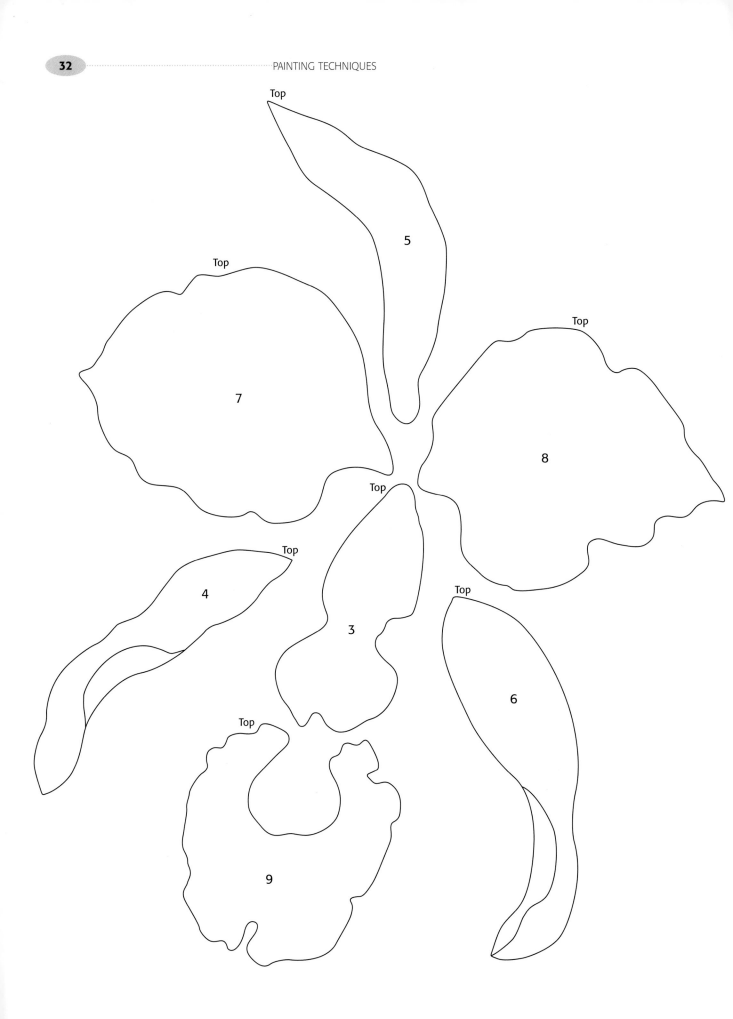

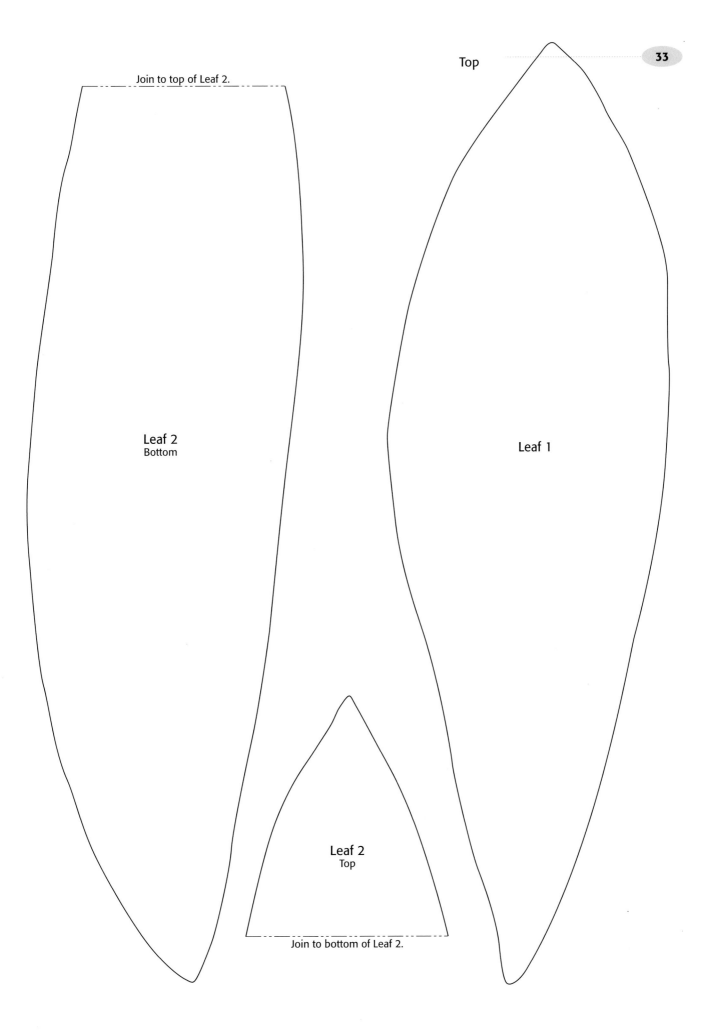

Join to top of Leaf 2.

Top

Leaf 2
Bottom

Leaf 1

Leaf 2
Top

Join to bottom of Leaf 2.

Resist was used on cotton to outline the elements of the design. The resist prevents the paint from spreading.

Resist was used with Jacquard textile paints on silk.

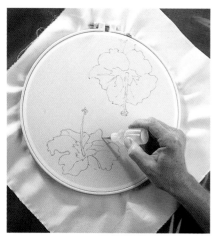

Step 3 of "Faux Batik: Painting with Resist"

Faux Batik: Painting with Resist

APPLYING RESIST TO FABRIC prevents the spread of the dye or paint. When the color hits the resist line, it is prevented from moving beyond it. The resist is washed out of the fabric after it has been dried and the paints are heat set. When resist is applied to a piece of white fabric, white lines will remain after the resist is washed out.

For best results when using resist, choose a smooth fabric. Draw your design with a water-soluble marking pen; then place the fabric in a plastic embroidery hoop or stretcher frame. Then place water-soluble resist in a small applicator bottle with a metal tip. Holding the bottle like a pen, draw over your design lines with the resist. Then, using brushes, paint inside the resist lines. The results are similar to batik, in which wax or starch is used as a resist, but without the waxy mess. This is a great way to achieve colorful, intricate designs.

The resist brand I prefer to use is Silkpaint. It goes on smoothly and rinses out with water. Mix five parts resist to one part water. After mixing, the resist will have air bubbles in it. I recommend mixing it the night before you want to use it so the bubbles dissolve and settle. The resist is then poured into a ½ -oz. applicator bottle. A plastic top pops into the top of the bottle and a metal tip is screwed over the plastic top. The metal tips come in three sizes. The medium tip, 7 mm, is easiest for beginners to use.

Materials

Smooth, evenly woven fabric
A line drawing, outlined in a permanent black marker
Fabric paints
Silkpaint resist and an applicator bottle with a 7-mm tip
Small paintbrushes
Plastic embroidery hoop or stretcher frame (It's okay if the design is
    larger than the hoop; it can be painted in sections.)
Water-soluble marking pen
Stencil tape
Measuring spoons and a plastic tray
Paper towels
Iron and ironing board
Plastic drop cloth

Directions

1. Tape the design to a smooth work surface. Tape fabric over the design and trace the design onto the fabric with the water-soluble marking pen. Remove the fabric and design from the work surface. Cover the table with the plastic drop cloth and tape it in place.
2. Place the fabric inside the embroidery hoop with the right side of the fabric facing up; place the hoop with the screw on top.
3. Using the applicator tip like a pen, draw over the design lines with the resist. The resist does not have to dry before you can paint.
4. Using measuring spoons and a plastic tray, mix the paint with equal

amounts of water. Dampen a small brush in water. Then test the color on a scrap of fabric. More water can be added to create lighter colors. Using a small amount of paint, start by painting in the middle of a large area, away from the resist lines. This allows you to see how much the paint is going to spread. Continue painting until all areas are covered.

5. Let the paint dry completely (at least 1 hour). Take the fabric out of the hoop. If your design is larger, reposition the hoop, apply the resist, and apply the paint. Allow to dry for 24 hours. I have found that if you let the paint or dye set for 24 hours, less color will rinse out of your fabric.

6. Lay paper towels over the fabric. Set the iron to the fabric setting you are using and press before rinsing. The paint must be heat set for 2 to 3 minutes before the resist is rinsed out of the fabric.

7. Soak the fabric in cold water for 20 minutes to dissolve the resist. Rinse in cool water and allow to dry.

Photo Transfer

THE PROCESS OF PHOTO TRANSFERRING involves copying an image onto transfer paper and pressing it onto fabric. For best results, choose a sharp photo or print that has contrasting colors. If you have the equipment, you can scan an image into your computer, print it on transfer paper, and press it onto fabric. I have done this, but I find print shops have higher-quality printers, and their presses are larger, resulting in better transfers.

I use photo-transferred images most often as appliqués (see "Appliqué" on page 47). Another way to use a photo-transferred image is to have the image pressed into a specific place on the fabric; then paint around and up to the image. The transfer edge acts like a resist, with paint stopping at its edge. The transfer looks more a part of the overall design, and you have eliminated the need to appliqué. This was the process I used for the Columbine and Hummingbird wall hanging (detail right).

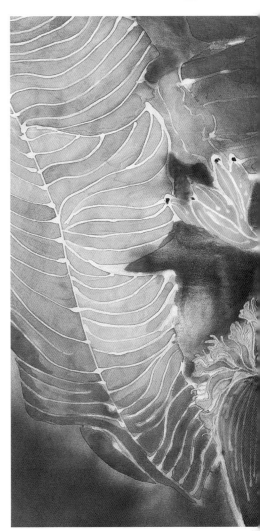

Banana leaf is drawn with resist and then painted with Setacolor.

This hummingbird was applied using the photo transfer method.

Tip

When painting around a transferred image, use diluted paint (equal parts water and paint). Adding more water than paint may cause the paint to run into the transferred image. If you want to use a watery color, apply resist (see page 13) around the image before you paint.

The butterfly on the left shows how the transferred image acts as a resist. Too much water added to the paint will cause the paint to bleed into the photo-transferred image as shown in the butterfly on the right.

Tip

If transferring the image with a household iron, leave a tab on the side of the image when cutting it out to make removal of the transfer paper easier. Be sure to fold the tab back, laying it over the image, so it is not pressed onto the fabric.

Materials

Smooth, thin fabric
Copyright-free image
Photo-transfer paper
Access to a photocopy machine
Air-soluble marker
Embroidery scissors or X-Acto knife and self-healing
　cutting mat or piece of glass
Paper, 8½" x 11"
Iron and ironing board (if necessary)

Directions

1. Photo-transfer paper is 8½" x 11", so arrange several images on a plain piece of paper the same size. I always print at least two copies of the same image, making one a little larger or changing the color (copy machines have a selection for making the image lighter or darker); then I choose the best one. Note that the image will be reversed once it is pressed onto the fabric.

2. After the images are printed onto the transfer paper, cut them out.

3. Using an air-soluble marker, mark the placement of the image on the fabric. Follow the manufacturer's recommendations for transferring the image. If required, take both the fabric and the transfer to the print shop and have them press it in place. Large designs cannot be transferred by a household iron; the steam holes create uneven pressure that results in an uneven transfer.

Stenciling

STENCILING IS OFTEN USED to create multiple images quickly. The designs can range from simple single-layer stencils to detailed multi-layer stencils. When using stencils, I apply color with either a foam sponge applicator or an airbrush. If you are stenciling by hand, it is best to use a thick paint, such as Novacolor. For intricate stencils, airbrushing produces the best results (see "Airbrushing" on page 36).

There are many ready-made stencils available. My favorite line of stencils is created by Diane Ericson. You can also create your own stencils, making them from either acetate or paper with a minimum of tools. When looking for a pattern for a single-layer stencil, think of simple, complete shapes with distinct outlines. For example, a butterfly may be six separate shapes: four wings, the head, and the body. Allow at least ⅛" of space between the shapes in the design. To stencil a more complex design, I make a multi-layer stencil consisting of a separate stencil for each color. If I plan to use the design only once or twice, I cut it out of paper. If I plan to use a design many times, I cut it from acetate so it can be cleaned and reused.

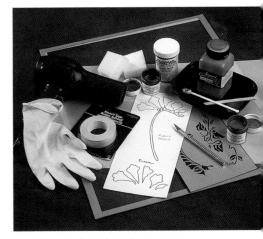

Stenciling tools and equipment

Paint was sponged over a trio of butterflies to create this design. The center design was painted separately.

Goldfinches and thistles were stenciled with an airbrush.

Cutting a stencil from paper

Cutting a stencil from acetate

Making Stencils

Materials

.005-mm clear acetate for acetate stencil
Design drawn on paper (or trace Butterfly Stencil below)
X-Acto knife and blade 11
Remount spray glue by 3M or other low-tack glue for acetate stencil
A piece of glass larger than your design
Stencil tape

Directions
Making a Single-Layer Stencil

1. Using a pencil, shade the areas of the design to be cut; allow about ⅛" between the pieces of the design. If you are making the stencil from acetate, spray the wrong side of the paper with glue and place the design, glue side down, onto the acetate

2. Tape the paper (or paper glued to acetate) onto the glass to keep it from shifting. With the X-Acto knife, cut out the shaded areas. If you cut into an area by mistake, cover it on both sides with tape to prevent paint from seeping through when you are stenciling. For points or corners, start cutting at the point and follow the design halfway. Then start at the point again and cut in the other direction.

Making a Multi-Layer Stencil

Follow the directions for "Making a Single-Layer Stencil." It is not necessary to allow ⅛" of space between the pieces of the design. Draw and cut a stencil for each color you will use in the design. To make sure the stencils for each color will line up, align the stencils and make a hole through all the stencils, punching one hole at the top right and one at the lower left. You can mark the holes of the first stencil on the fabric with an air-soluble marker and line up the holes of each remaining stencil.

Butterfly Stencil

Stenciling with a Foam Sponge

Materials
Smooth fabric
Water-soluble paints, such as Versatex, Novacolor, or Createx
Foam sponge or dense foam, such as a pillow form, cut in 2" squares
Stencil
Stencil tape
Plastic disposable tray or plate
Scrap paper for practice
Plastic drop cloth

Directions
1. Cover a table with the plastic drop cloth and tape the plastic in place.
2. Spoon a small amount of paint into a plastic tray or plate. Wad the foam into a ball and dab it into the paint. Sponge onto paper, making sure the paint is distributed evenly. Practice stenciling on paper, printing lightly with a small amount of paint.
3. Press the fabric and lay it on top of the table. Tape down the corners of the fabric to prevent it from shifting. Anchor the stencil onto the fabric with stencil tape.
4. Lightly sponge paint onto the fabric with an up-and-down motion. Let the paint dry for a minute, remove the stencil, reposition, and repeat.

> **Tip**
>
> For thin silks, press the wrong side of the fabric onto the waxy side of freezer paper before stenciling. The freezer paper keeps the fabric smooth and flat while you apply the paint.

Step 4 of "Stenciling with a Foam Sponge"

> **Tip**
>
> Acetate stencils should be cleaned after two to three uses to prevent paint that is on the stencil from smearing onto the fabric. Soak the stencil in soapy water when you are finished. Place the stencil over paper towels and pat dry. Do not rub the stencil; you could tear it. Dry and store flat.

The flower and berry motifs on these table linens were created with stencils.

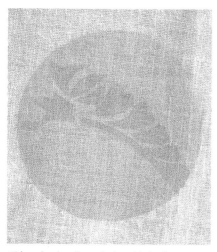

Airbrushed yellow circle with leaf stenciled over the top

Stenciling variations with one stencil

Stenciling with an Airbrush

Materials

Materials as listed on page 40 except for foam sponge and plastic tray
Airbrush
Air compressor
Follow steps 1 and 3 for "Stenciling with a Foam Sponge" on page 39; then refer to "Airbrushing" on page 41 to apply the color.

Designing with Stencils

Diane Ericson has created beautiful garments with stencils. She achieves dimensional results by painting layers of stencils. First stencil a simple shape, such as a circle; then stencil a detailed image over it.

You can use portions of stencils by taping paper or acetate over sections. I love the endless possibilities—you can flip the stencil over, use portions of it, rotate it, mask off sections—for creating a variety of designs from one stencil.

Another idea Diane uses is to create a shadow by using a portion of the same stencil, offset and stenciled lightly.

Stenciling allows you to duplicate a detailed design accurately; however, repeating the same pattern over and over can cause the eye to lose interest. To stimulate interest, cut several stencils per subject and use them in different combinations. This allows the design to change but still gives you the benefit of creating quickly. This technique was used on the "Goldfinch and Thistle" quilt (page 42).

Lizard and butterfly on wool crepe. A shadow is created below the lizard by offsetting the stencil and applying less paint. The same technique was used to create the second wing of the butterfly.

Airbrushing

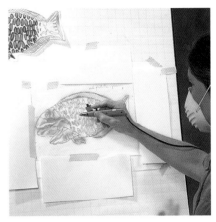

A N **AIRBRUSH IS EASIER TO USE** than you would think. The paint mixes with compressed air to produce tiny dots of paint. You hold an airbrush like a pen, using your index finger to release the trigger, which in turn disperses a mixture of air and paint. The results are instant—a soft spray of color. This technique can be used on any fabric. My favorite airbrush is from Aztek because it is lightweight and easy to use and clean. The body is guaranteed for life. Stencils are a great way to control the placement of paint, allowing you to create detailed designs (see "Stenciling" on page 38).

Airbrushing

Tips for Airbrushing

1. Usually the compressor is set at 35–40 pounds per square inch (PSI) for an airbrush. PSI is used to measure the air pressure in the tank and in the hose from the tank to the airbrush.

2. Make sure your compressor allows you to release water, which can clog your airbrush. Usually there is a drain valve on the bottom of the tank.

3. I use paint specified for airbrushing and always dilute it with the same brand of extender: 50% paint, 50% extender. Createx has a great line of paints suitable for fabric in both transparent and opaque colors.

4. Always start by spraying on paper. If the airbrush is clogged or the color you just used is still in the tip, the mistake will happen on the paper, not on your fabric.

Hold an airbrush like a pen.

5. On most airbrushes, the top of the paint cap will have a hole to release air. It must remain open and free of dried paint.

6. If you are using a stencil, tape it in place with low-tack drafting or stencil tape. Then tape paper around the stencil to prevent overspray. If the stencil is large and detailed, spray the back of the stencil with a low-tack glue that allows you to reposition the stencil. This will keep the stencil flat against the fabric and prevent spray from getting under the stencil.

7. The most common problem is paint drying over the tip. Remove the paint from the cup, put in airbrush cleaner, and spray. Brush away any excess paint that remains on the tip with a soft brush, such as an old toothbrush.

8. If you will not be using the airbrush for more than 30 minutes, remove the paint cup and clean the airbrush tip.

The parrot fish is airbrushed by using a different stencil for each color of paint.

Designing with an Airbrush

Torn paper makes a nice uneven edge for skies and landscapes. Simply tear several sheets of paper to create a variety of edges. Hold the torn edge against the fabric and spray along the edge. Alternate the sheets of paper to create a landscape or background.

Airbrushed landscape from torn-paper stencils.

THE DESIGN PROCESS
Design Inspiration

MOST IMPORTANT IN DEVELOPING a design is allowing yourself the freedom to experiment. Test out ideas, techniques, and colors on a scrap. It's the best way to learn. We all want masterpieces, but you have to be willing to take chances to learn and grow as an artist.

Study and observe artwork of others. I have learned so much by looking at wildlife paintings and reading tips from the artists. I keep my favorite books handy, so that when I am at a loss of which direction to take, I can quickly search for answers and ideas. *The Creative Artist: A Fine Artist's Guide to Expanding Your Creativity and Achieving Your Artistic Potential* by Nita Leland is a good resource.

Goldfinch and Thistle

My inspiration for the goldfinch and thistles came while running in a state park in Ohio. On my run, I saw a field of thistle. As I was looking out at the field, a pair of goldfinches flew out to the flowers. I fell in love with the color combination of the purple thistle and the yellow, black, and white bird. I decided to combine the images in one design. In order to give myself several design options, I created three views of the bird and cut stencils for each. I also made several stencils of thistle leaves and two different stencils for the thistle flowers. I combined the stencils in various combinations to make three different designs as seen here and opposite.

This Goldfinch and Thistle design was turned into a quilted wall hanging and machine embroidered for added detail. A leaf-printed border with stenciled acorns frames the design (see "Leaf Printing" on page 28).

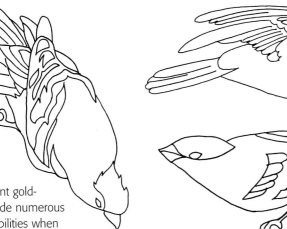

These acorn stencils were used for the border on the quilt shown opposite.

Three different gold-finches provide numerous design possibilities when combined with the thistle flowers.

Each of these thistle pieces was cut as a separate stencil, then used in a variety of design combinations.

The same thistle and goldfinch stencils were used to create two additional airbrushed designs.

Banana and Lizard

T O **START YOUR DESIGN,** choose a photo or image that you are excited about. I encourage you to do some research and learn more about the subject you are going to paint. For example, I wanted to use the banana flower in a design. I found photos of it, ranging in colors from peach to purple. This gave me more freedom when it came time to paint. I also learned it is really called a "head," not a "flower"!

If you can observe your subject with your own eyes, it will make an even stronger impact. Much of my work is a combination of research (through books and magazines), and observation (in nature). I am lucky enough to have a

Sketch of banana head

Banana head and leaves on silk

mother-in-law that is an avid gardener, so I went to her house and created a quick sketch of a banana head.

I redrew the design, adding bananas to the stalk. Because banana leaves are really large, I drew several individual leaves on separate sheets of 11" x 14" paper. I arranged them around the stalk, taping them in place. Finally, I added a lizard to the stalk.

Once I had the design created, I experimented with different painting techniques. I highly recommend working out your ideas on inexpensive cotton or silk at this point. I originally painted the lizard with Setacolor but no resist. The results looked sloppy, with blurry edges. So, I cut a stencil of the lizard. I airbrushed several lizards onto a scrap of fabric and was happy with the results.

After I airbrushed the lizard, I applied resist around the edges of the lizard and over the design lines of the stalk, flowers, and leaves. I then painted the design with Setacolor.

I really liked my initial design, so I decided to paint it again, this time with metallic Lumiere paints as a resist. I had been painting with Lumiere for years, but this was the first time I attempted to use it as a resist. I tried it and was surprised at the thin, delicate lines I could create. I simply poured the paint into the resist bottle and used a 7-mm tip. (See "Faux Batik: Painting with Resist" on page 34).

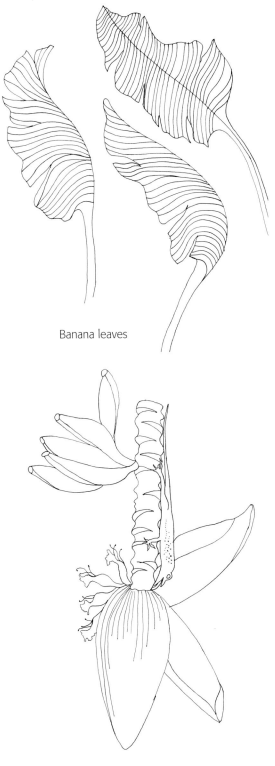

Banana leaves

To create the banana stalk, Copper Lumiere is used as a resist.

Completed banana stalk and lizard

Design Development

Designing in Sections

THE EASIEST WAY TO CREATE detailed work is to paint in sections and sew the pieces together to make a larger design. This gives you the freedom to make mistakes and changes. If you don't like part of the design, you can simply repaint that one section. Just knowing this can make you feel more relaxed.

In the "Heron with Frog" wall hanging, the sky, heron, plants, and beach were created on one piece of silk with an airbrush and stencils. The water below was dyed with Colorhue and the scrunch, dip, and dye method. Then the two pieces were joined together. The frog was painted separately and appliquéd in place (see "Appliqué" on page 47).

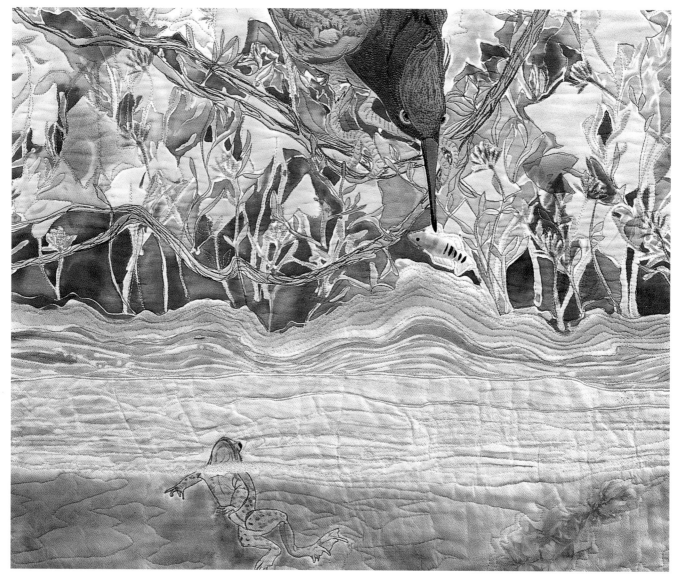

Heron with Frog by Ginny Eckley, 1998, Houston, Texas, 28" x 36".

Appliqué

One way to create designs with painted fabric is to paint a pattern on the fabric and cut an appliqué shape from the patterned area. This gives you design flexibility and allows you to choose the best areas of the painted fabric for your appliqué images, rather than having to paint a perfect image from the start.

When making complex designs, you can also paint some of the elements on separate pieces of fabric and experiment until you achieve the desired result. When you are satisfied with your design elements, you can cut them out and use them for appliqués on a painted background. This is the concept that Joan and I used for the hand-painted orchid in "Hand Painting with Setacolor" on page 30.

You can use one of the following methods to appliqué your painted designs by hand or machine.

Hand Appliqué by Joan Toomey

I prefer to use YLI silk thread, 100 weight, for the orchid shown on page 30. This thread just disappears into the fabric. An alternative is machine-embroidery thread in 50-weight cotton. Choose colors that match the painted edges of each piece. The disadvantage of matching the colors is that you need to have a large variety of colors.

Select a needle with a fine shaft, such as a #12 appliqué needle, milliner's needle, or straw needle. A needle with a thicker shaft tends to pull the threads apart.

Materials

Background fabric
Appliqué fabrics prepared as
    specified on page 31
100-weight silk thread (YLI light
    taupe #242 and dark taupe
    #235) or 50-weight cotton
    machine-embroidery thread
Fine needle (#12 appliqué)
Quilter's or soapstone pencil
Pins

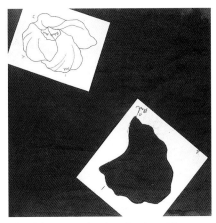

This fabric was dyed and painted for "Poppies" by Barbara Wenders. First a poppy was drawn; then an enlarged pattern for each petal was cut from paper. To create the petals, the petal pattern is placed over the fabric and moved around until the desired look is achieved; then it is taped in place. The pattern is traced; then 1/4" seam allowances are added. The process is repeated for each petal of the flower. Finally, each of the petals are cut out and appliquéd in place on a background fabric.

Orchid, hand appliquéd by Joan Toomey

Tip

Crisp fabrics appliqué easily. Use spray starch to make soft fabrics crisp.

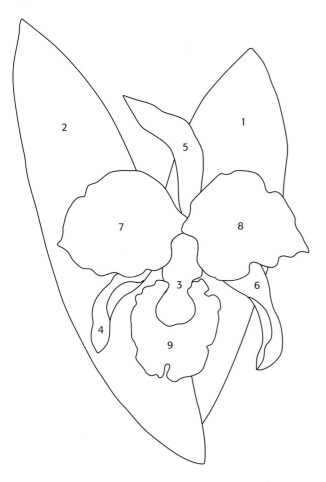

Directions

1. Lightly trace around each design piece on the right side of the appliqué fabric with a quilter's or soapstone pencil. This is the stitching line. Draw a second line, ¼" away from the stitching line. Cut each piece along the outer marked line.

2. Lightly trace the perimeter of the pattern lines onto the background fabric to guide the placement of the pattern pieces.

3. Pin and sew one piece at a time. For appliqué pieces that overlap, start with the bottom piece first. It is helpful to number the appliqué pieces in the order that they should be stitched in place. Pin the first appliqué piece to the background fabric. Fold the seam allowance under as you sew. Bring your needle up through the background fabric, just catching the very edge of the appliqué. Hold the seam allowance under with your non-stitching hand. Place your index finger on the back of the fabric and your thumbnail on top of the appliqué piece as if it were a pin. Turn the fabric under, using your needle to gently push the seam allowance under.

> ### Tip
> If the fabric doesn't turn easily, you can wet the needle slightly to help grab the fabric.

Machine Appliqué

Materials
Background fabric
Appliqué fabrics prepared as specified on page 00.
Pink, yellow, purple, and green machine-embroidery thread
White cotton machine-basting thread or cotton embroidery thread
Machine-embroidery needle, size 75
Lightweight fusible web
Tear-away stabilizer
Sewing machine with darning or free-motion foot
Pins
Iron and ironing board

Orchid, machine appliquéd by Ginny Eckley

Directions for Machine Setup

1. Wind a bobbin spool with cotton thread. (I use white because it produces the least amount of lint.)
2. Insert a new #75 needle. Lower the top tension one full number. Keep the feed dogs up.
3. Place the darning foot on the machine. Draw up the bobbin thread. Set the stitch to a medium width zigzag stitch.

Directions for Fabric Preparation

1. Rough-cut fusible web for the appliqué fabrics. Following the manufacturer's directions, press fusible web onto the wrong side of the fabric. Cut along the pattern line of each piece. Remove the paper backing.
2. Press the appliqué pieces onto the background; for pieces that overlap, place the bottom pieces on the background first.
3. Pin the stabilizer to the wrong side of the background fabric.
4. Stitch along the edges of each appliqué piece with closely spaced zigzag stitches. Change the thread color in the needle as necessary. Use straight stitches to draw design lines on the interior of appliqués (see "Machine Embroidery" on page 50).

> **Tip**
>
> The glues from fusible webs can seep through silk fabrics and show through, giving them a plastic look. For best results, back your silk appliqué pieces with interfacing. A lightweight iron-on interfacing, such as Touch of Gold or 911F Pellon, works well for backing silk fabrics.

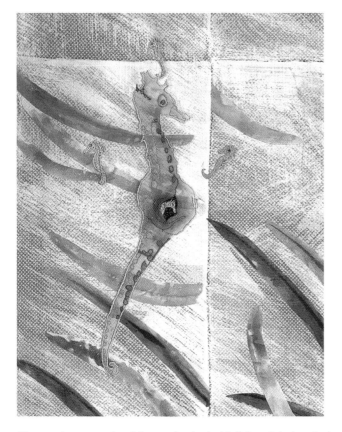 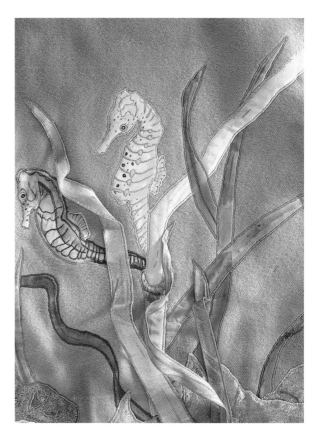

The sea horse on the right was backed with lightweight interfacing to eliminate the plastic look and prevent show-through; the sea horse on the left was fused without using interfacing.

Machine Embroidery

I love combining painting with machine embroidery. I often take the main design elements and add quite a bit of stitching to them. Using free-motion embroidery allows you to move the fabric under the machine in any direction.

Goldfinches were airbrushed onto silk through a stencil; then the fabric was layered over fleece. The top two birds were embellished with free-motion stitching.

> ### Tip
>
> ### Combining Appliqué with Free-Motion Embroidery
>
> After the painted image has been heat set, and before it is cut out, back the image with lightweight interfacing. Following the manufacturer's directions, cut a piece of fusible web and apply it to the interfacing. Cut the image out. Remove the paper from the web and press the image onto your background fabric. Layer the fleece and backing behind your painted design. Pin or baste the layers together.
>
> When using the free-motion foot and machine-embroidery thread, straight stitch around the edge of the image. Using thread to match the color of the image, stitch around the edges. Use small zigzag stitches that are close together. If you are stitching around a bird, change thread colors as you move from the yellow beak to the blue feathers. This way the image will look more like a part of the piece, rather than like an appliqué.

Directions
1. Place the darning or free-motion foot on the machine. The foot has a built-in spring that allows you to stitch in all directions.
2. Place white cotton embroidery or cotton basting thread in the bobbin. (White thread creates the least amount of lint.)
3. Place a 75 "Sharp," or machine-embroidery needle, in the machine.
4. Thread the machine with the desired machine-embroidery thread. Loosen the top tension one full number. This allows the top thread to be the dominant thread. If the bobbin thread shows on top, loosen it an additional half number.
5. Stitch over your painted image as desired.

GALLERY

Arizona Mountains by Ginny Eckley, 1999, 58" x 50". A spring trip to the mountains and deserts of Arizona was the inspiration behind this piece. I was delighted at all the cactus and wildflowers in bloom. The land was alive with birds, but it was the Gila woodpecker that I found most attractive. The beautiful red rock in various formations was so captivating, I found myself just gazing out into the mountains for hours. The techniques used were painting with resist, painting on plastic, airbrushing, and free-motion embroidery.

Heron with Frog by Ginny Eckley, 1998, Houston, Texas, 28" x 36". Perching on a branch, a heron catches a fish in his long, sharp beak. Below them, a frog watches intently. The sky, heron, plants, and beach were created on one piece of silk with an airbrush and stencils. The frog was painted on a separate piece of silk with Setacolor and markers and appliquéd to the design background. Silkpaint resist and Colorhue dyes were used on China silk to create the surface water patterns. The water below the frog's head was created by scrunching and dipping the fabric into Colorhue dyes.

Lotus in Akita Park I by Ginny Eckley, 1998, Houston, Texas, 22" x 46". A frog lifts its head through the waters, into the sunlight. In deeper, darker waters, fish swim among the lotus leaves. Each of the leaves, pods, and flowers was painted and embroidered separately and machine appliquéd to the background. The lotus leaves were airbrushed. Other design elements were painted with Colorhue and Silkpaint resist. The silk crepe background was dyed with Colorhue dyes and the scrunch, dip, and dye method. The green stems were cut from Japanese kimono fabric and appliquéd with a blind-hem stitch.

Lotus in Akita Park II by Ginny Eckley, 1998, Houston, Texas, 19" x 36". Lotus flowers and leaves stand tall in a Japanese pond. A dragonfly barely escapes the grasp of a frog, as another dragonfly rests on a lotus flower. The dragonflies were created by embroidering through layers of tulle. Other techniques used in this wall hanging are the same as those used for Lotus in Akita Park 1.

Salmon on the Rocks by Ginny Eckley, 1996, Houston, Texas, 51" x 54". The salmon begins its journey as a bright, round egg nestled amongst rocks in a riverbed. It breaks through its shell and is born with a pouch that provides nourishment. This design was created in sections and machine appliquéd together. The fish were painted with Colorhue, fabric markers, and Lumiere paints and machine appliquéd over the rocks and water. The rocks were painted on silk taffeta. The water is marbleized silk, layered with tulle (see Judy Simmons's book *Creative Marbling on Fabric*). Leaves at the top edge of the water are cut from a piece of China silk that was painted with Setacolor and sprinkled with salt. The flowers were cut from yellow cotton.

Salmon over the Waterfall by Ginny Eckley, 1996, Houston, Texas, 51" x 54". After a year or so in the streams, the salmon migrate to the ocean, just after the spring rains. The design was painted and dyed on different silks with Colorhue, fabric markers, and Lumiere paints. The rocks were painted on dry-cleaning bags with Colorhue dyes. The lower section of water was created with Silkpaint resist and Colorhue. The waterfalls were painted with white Lumiere paint and embellished with silk thread. The crepe background was dyed using Colorhue and the scrunch, dip, and dye method.

The Final Journey by Ginny Eckley, 1997, Houston, Texas, 51" x 54". The salmon undergo drastic physical changes as they head upstream to the place where their life began. The female is shown digging a redd, or nest, to deposit her eggs. Within days, the Pacific salmon die. The lower water was painted on crepe with Silkpaint resist and Colorhue dyes. Large rocks at the ocean's edge were painted on dry-cleaning bags with Colorhue. The stream was created from green marbleized silk (see Judy Simmons's book *Creative Marbling on Fabric*). Real leaves and plants were painted and pressed along the stream's edge. All the fish were painted separately and machine embroidered in place. Setacolor and salt were used to achieve some of the fish patterns.

Roseate Spoonbill by Ginny Eckley, 1998, Houston, Texas, 60" x 84". A roseate spoonbill is about to land in the field close to the water's edge. Behind him is a group of herons preening. A flock of cranes flies overhead. This wall hanging was created with airbrushing on layers of upholstery fabric. Details were added with fabric markers and Lumiere paint. The birds were airbrushed with paper stencils, and the plants and water patterns were airbrushed with plastic stencils.

Herons by Ginny Eckley, 1998, Houston, Texas, 36" x 84". Two graceful herons relax in shallow water. In the distance, a heron is fishing for food. This design was airbrushed on synthetic upholstery fabric. Fabric markers and Lumiere paint were used to add details. Paper stencils were used for the birds. Plastic stencils were cut for the plants and water patterns.

It's a Jungle Out There by Joan Toomey, 1997, Herndon, Virginia, 36" x 48". This design was hand painted with Setacolor in sections on bright-colored cotton. The pieces were hand appliquéd onto a black cotton background.

Isabel's Fantasy Garden I by Joan Toomey, 1998, Herndon, Virginia, 36" x 48". This piece was inspired by a pen-and-ink doodle from a wonderful artist, Isabel Stapko. It was painted with Setacolor on various colors of fine cotton. Markers were used to create detail. It was embellished with beads to re-create the details in the original pen-and-ink design.

Isabel's Fantasy Garden II by Joan Toomey, 1999, Herndon, Virginia, 76" x 24". "This piece is dedicated to Isabel Stapko, whom I admired tremendously. We became instant friends during a hand-appliqué class I was teaching. She recently died of cancer, and I miss her."

Iris by Carol Ann Matthews, 1999, Canton, Michigan, 24" x 30". "Inspired from my garden, these iris were hand painted and machine appliquéd onto a painted cotton background. I was delighted to find a border that so closely matched the iris I painted."

Forget-me-nots by Carol Ann Matthews, 1999, Canton, Michigan, 24" x 27". "I drew the flowers from my garden, then brought them to life with paint." The border is designed to mimic the lattice pattern in Carol's garden. Hand-dyed cotton fabrics behind the lattice bring the background colors into the border.

Fable of the Four Friends by Myrna Schatzman, 1999, Great Falls, Virginia, 35" x 24". This design was inspired by a fifteenth-century Persian miniature. It is painted with Setacolor on cotton, hand appliquéd, and hand embroidered.

Anniversary Hollyhocks by
Katherine Crerar, 1999,
Vienna, Virginia, 24" x 44".
"This design is an adaptation
of a photograph taken on our
fortieth-wedding-anniversary
trip." It is hand painted, hand
appliquéd, beaded, and
quilted.

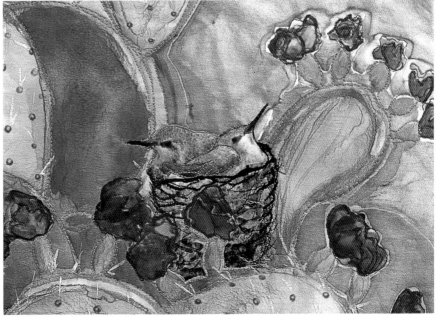

Hummingbird Nestled in Cactus by Ginny Eckley, 1999, Houston, Texas, 25½" x 19¾". The cactus is one of my favorite plants, as it survives in harsh conditions. With its beautiful flowers, it makes a stunning home for the hummingbirds. It is painted with Setacolor, markers, and Lumiere. The bird nest is photocopied and then machine-embroidered. Flowers are placed over the nest to camouflage It.

COLORHUE-DYED SCARF

Lightweight China silk works best for this project. The thinner the fabric, the better the dye will penetrate.

Materials

Hemmed scarf
Colorhue dyes
1" foam brushes, 1 for each dye color
10" length of PVC pipe*
X-Acto knife
Polyester thread
Stencil tape
Plastic cups for mixing dye and a plastic plate
Disposable gloves
Plastic drop cloth
Masking tape

*To determine the circumference of pipe you need, fold over a corner of the scarf, aligning adjacent edges and creating a diagonal line. Measure the length of the diagonal and add 2". For an 8"-wide scarf, my diagonal measurement was 11", so I bought a pipe with a 13" circumference.

Claire Teagan of Michigan creates beautiful Shibori-like patterns with Colorhue, PVC pipe, and thread. This scarf is one of her creations.

This silk Shibori scarf by Claire started out off-white. It was colored with black, pink, blue, and green dye and given sheen with a metallic wash of Lumiere paint.

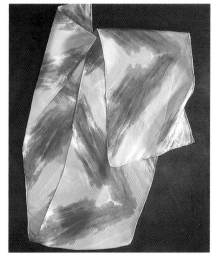

Colorhue dye in blue and yellow was used to create this scarf.

Step 2 of "Colorhue-Dyed Scarf"

Step 3 of "Colorhue-Dyed Scarf"

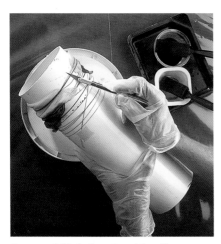

Step 4 of "Colorhue-Dyed Scarf"

Directions

1. Measure the width of the scarf. If your scarf is 9", fold the end of the scarf over 9". Continue folding the fabric back and forth at 9" intervals to roughly make a square; fold over any excess at end. Fold the square in half diagonally, creating a triangle. Lay the long edge of the scarf triangle over the pipe, about 1" from one edge of the pipe. Anchor the ends of the triangle with small pieces of tape. There should be a 1" space of pipe kept open, where the scarf ends do not touch each other.

2. Starting at the long edge of the triangle, wrap thread around the pipe once and knot the thread. Wrap a few more times and remove the tape. Continue wrapping the thread around the triangle on the pipe, spacing each wrap about ¼" apart. Push the silk down, creating ribs. Continue in this manner until the whole silk triangle is wrapped with thread.

3. Cover the table with plastic and put on your gloves. Mix equal amounts of Colorhue dye and water into a cup. Hold the pipe over the plastic plate and apply the dye to the silk with a foam brush, pushing the dyes into the silk. Continue painting, changing colors as desired. When finished, stand the pipe up, allowing the scarf to dry for at least 1 hour.

4. Using the X-Acto knife, cut the threads on the pipe between the ends of the silk triangle. Unfold the silk. If you want more color, simply refold and repeat the process. When finished, rinse in cool water.

Colorhue-Dyed Scarf with Metallic Wash

Materials

Same as for Colorhue-Dyed Scarf as listed on page 65, plus Lumiere paint

Directions

Complete steps 1–3 above. Let the scarf dry; then brush with a Lumiere wash. Make the wash by mixing five parts water to one part Lumiere paint. Practice on a scrap piece of silk. When you achieve the desired result, apply the wash to the right side of your silk with a brush; allow to dry.

Tip

Scrunch and Twist Method

For very long scarves or strips of fabric, after you have wrapped 4" of the fabric with thread as in step 2 above, push the fabric down and twist at the same time, scrunching it together. This is how Claire achieved the pattern in her scarves on page 65.

SILK BLOUSE SPONGE-PAINTED WITH RESIST

This technique is great for overdyeing fabric or clothing, and it works on all weights of silk. It is a perfect technique for a blouse that has a permanent stain or spot! Sponge resist onto silk and add dye to create bubbles of color.

Materials

Silk blouse or fabric
Colorhue dye or Setasilk paint
Silkpaint resist
2 plastic dry-cleaning bags
Foam board
Sea sponges
Small plastic trays
Disposable gloves
Plastic hanger
Masking tape
Iron and ironing board
Hair dryer (optional)
Small brushes
Plastic drop cloth

Directions

NOTE: Refer to the general directions for "Sponge Painting" on page 25.

1. Cover the table with the plastic drop cloth and tape the plastic in place. Cut the foam board to fit inside the blouse. Cover it with a plastic bag, taping the plastic in place.
2. Thin resist by mixing with an equal amount of water. Mix thoroughly and pour into a tray. Dip a sponge into the resist; then dab resist onto the silk. Wherever you want to keep the original color, sponge on the resist.
3. Put on gloves. You can add color immediately; the resist does not have to dry first. Color can be sponged on or painted on with small brushes for more control. Since the resist is diluted, some of the dye will break through the resist, creating veins of color.
4. Work in sections, allowing each section to dry before moving on. A hair dryer can be used to speed up the drying process, but set it on cool.
5. Place a plastic bag over the hanger. Place the blouse on the hanger, over the plastic. This will allow it to dry without the dyes bleeding from front to back. Hang for 24 hours to dry.
6. Soak the blouse in cool water about 20 minutes to soften the resist. Then rub, rinse, and hang to dry. Press with an iron on each side for 30 seconds to set the dye.

WISTERIA BLOUSE

For the wisteria design that highlights the shoulder area of this blouse, I used Setacolor without resist. The resist keeps the paint from spreading, providing a safeguard. The choice to use the resist or not is yours!

Materials

Blouse, prewashed and pressed
Fleece, flat and dense
Blue, purple, and green transparent fabric paints
Silkpaint resist in applicator with 7-mm tip (optional)
Small brushes
Air-soluble or water-soluble marker
Pins
Scrap of fabric to test design and color
Small tray or containers for paints
Iron and ironing board
Fabric markers (optional)
Hair dryer (optional)
Paper

Directions

1. Trace or photocopy the wisteria patterns on pages 71–73 onto paper.
2. Slip the pattern for the back under the back of the blouse and trace it with the air-soluble or water-soluble marker. Rotate the pattern or use portions of the pattern as desired. Extensions of leaves and buds can be used to lengthen or widen the pattern if desired.
3. Cut fleece to fit on the inside of the blouse. Slip under the back of the blouse and pin; keep pins about 1" away from the design.
4. For crisp edges, trace the outlines of the flowers and leaves with the resist. The resist does not have to dry before you paint. For a softer look, eliminate this step.
5. Paint the flowers first, using both blue and purple transparent paints. Start by mixing the paint with an equal amount of water. Then place some of the mixed paint into another container and add more water to create a lighter shade of the same color.
6. Once you have mixed the purple and blue paint, create a test piece. Draw part of the wisteria on your scrap fabric; then test the colors and consistency of the paint. Always start in the center of a flower or petal, letting the paint spread. If your paint is spreading too quickly, going outside the lines, you can switch to a smaller brush or add more paint to your mix.
7. You can paint some of the leaves over the flowers, creating a more dimensional design. The effect will be quite soft. Again, begin by mixing the paint as described in step 5. For narrow areas, such as the stem, use a liner brush. Fabric markers can also be used to add fine lines and details.
8. Let dry thoroughly. You can speed the drying process with a hair dryer set on a cool setting. Repeat this process for the front of the blouse with the wisteria pattern on page 71.
9. Set the paint by pressing on the wrong side for 2 to 3 minutes. If you used resist, soak in cool water for 20 minutes after heat setting. Rinse in cool water and hang to dry.

Tip

For a darker line that defines the edges, use a liner brush. Wet it first, squeeze out the excess water, and then dip the tip of the brush into the undiluted paint. This works great along the edge of a petal or leaf.

Back of blouse

Wisteria Blouse
Front

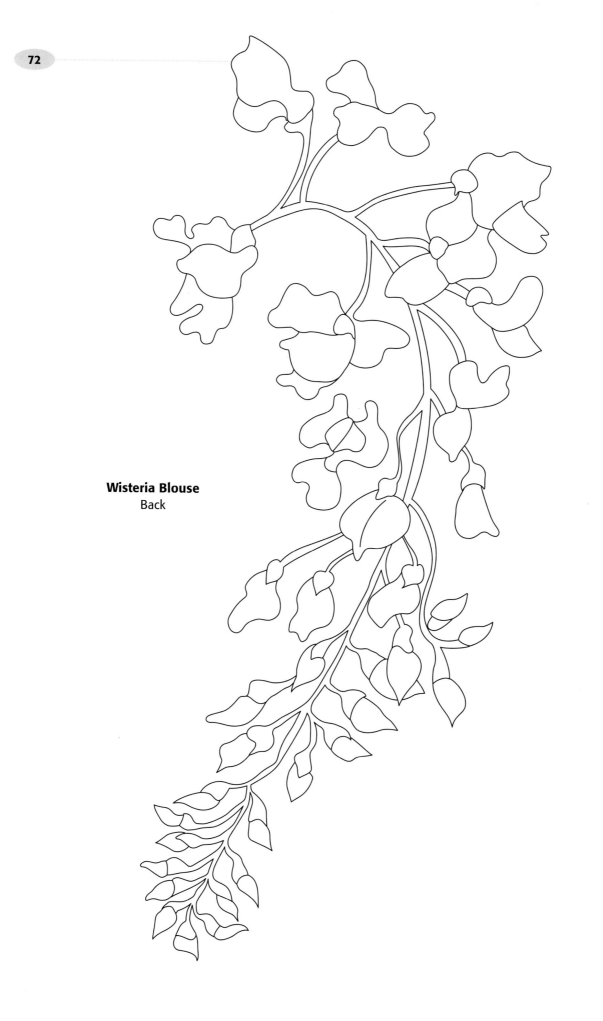

Wisteria Blouse
Back

Wisteria Blouse
Leaves and buds to lengthen or widen wisteria

HIBISCUS AND HUMMINGBIRD PILLOW

The center panel of the pillow was created with resist and Setacolor paints. The borders were dyed with Colorhue dyes and the scrunch, dip, and dye method.

Materials

14" x 14" square of prewashed white silk fabric for pillow top
(I used silk charmeuse, 23 mm.)

14" x 14" square of coordinating fabric for pillow back

14" x 18" piece of fleece

⅝ yd. silk fabric for borders (I used lime green China silk.)

1 yd. lightweight fusible interfacing

18"-square pillow form

4 decorative buttons, ¾" diameter

Setacolor transparent colors: 17 lemon yellow, 18 pernod yellow, 21 orange, 22 bengale pink, 28 moss green, 30 turquoise, 14 velvet brown, 20 red ochre, 19 black lake

Setacolor opaque colors: 44 pearl and 45 gold

Colorhue colors: yellow and turquoise for pillow border

Silkpaint resist in applicator with medium (7-mm) tip

Brushes ranging from a #2 liner brush to a 1" brush

Containers with lids to mix and store paint

A set of measuring spoons to mix paint and water

10" plastic embroidery hoop

Air-soluble or water-soluble marking pen with fine tip

Tracing paper

Low-tack tape, such as stencil or drafting tape

Hair dryer

Iron and ironing board

Towel

Fabric markers (optional)

Pins

Directions
Painting the Flowers

1. Trace or photocopy the pattern on pages 79–82 onto paper; tape paper together as necessary for a complete design. Tape the pattern to the table. Center the white silk over the pattern. Tape the corners of the fabric to the table. For now, trace only the 2 hibiscus flowers. Use the air- or water-soluble marking pen.

2. Remove the tape from the fabric. Place the plain ring of the embroidery hoop on the table. Lay the fabric over the hoop with the flowers in the center. Place the hoop with the screw on top. Adjust the screw to tighten. For the flowers, you will be using Setacolor numbers 17, 21, 22, and 44.

3. For a crisp edge, outline the outside edges of the flowers with resist. The resist will stop the paint and create a white line where it is applied, as in batik. Make sure the resist has no broken lines, or the paint will flow outside the petals. An alternative to the resist is to paint the petal edges with undiluted paint and a liner brush.

4. With a fine-point liner brush and undiluted pink, paint the dots of the stigma, which are at the top of the stamen. Next, mix a small amount of the same color with an equal amount of water. Use this to paint the center of the flowers.

> **Tip**
>
> Do not overload your brushes. The paint will drip, or spread outside the area you are painting. I dip the tip of my brush into the paint and then dab it over the outside edge of the container or on a paper towel, removing any excess paint.

Flowers painted on white silk

5. Mix 1 part yellow paint to 3 parts water. Using a ½" brush, start in the center of the petals and let the paint spread. Since orange will be painted over this, it does not need to be painted evenly. The yellow paint acts as an undertone.

6. Leave the fabric in the hoop and tape the corners of the fabric to the table. Dry the yellow paint with the hair dryer. If the fabric is not taped down, the hair dryer can blow the edges of the fabric into the wet paint.

7. Mix 2 parts orange paint to 1 part water. Paint the petals as in step 5; allow to dry.

8. Mix 1 part pink to 3 parts water. If you have paint left from step 4, just add water to it. Use the liner brush to draw vein lines from the center out to the petal edges. Create a shadow around the center by painting next to the center and out about ⅛". Allow to dry.

9. Paint the stamen with the liner brush and opaque pearl. If you have placed resist over the stamen, it can be repainted or touched up after the painting is complete and the resist is rinsed out (see "Painting the Background" on page 77, step 3).

10. Paint the dots of pollen with undiluted yellow and the liner brush. Dry both flowers and remove the fabric from the hoop.

Painting the Hummingbird

1. Trace the hummingbird onto the fabric in the same manner as you traced the hibiscus flowers. Place the fabric in the hoop with the bird in the center. Tape the corners of the fabric to the table.

2. Using the resist, draw around the outside edge of the bird and the flower next to the bird, including the stamen. Fill in the white sections of the tail feathers with resist.

3. Mix 1 part pernod yellow to 2 parts water. Using a ½" flat brush and starting in the center of the body, paint the body, head, and upper wings.

4. Use the liner brush and undiluted red ochre to create feather lines in the wings. Dry; then mix 1 part red ochre to 3 parts water; paint the wings and top of the head near the beak.

5. Mix 1 part orange to 1 part water; paint the orange section of the tail feathers.

6. Mix 1 part brown to 1 part water; paint the brown section of the tail feathers.

7. Mix 1 part turquoise to 1 part water; paint a small scallop pattern randomly over the body. (Fabric markers can also be used, but the fabric must be dry or the marker lines will spread.)

8. If desired, you may tone down the green body with a paint wash. Mix 1 part red ochre or brown to 4 parts water. Since the paint mixture is mostly water, start at the center of the body and let it spread out.

9. Using the liner brush and black, paint the eye and beak. (Again, markers can be used for this if you prefer.)

10. Dry the bird with the hair dryer on the cool setting. Mix 1 part gold to 3 parts water. Using a ½" flat brush, start at the center and paint lightly, over all but the beak. Dry the fabric and remove it from the hoop.

Hummingbird and hibiscus

Painting the Leaves

1. Lightly press the fabric to remove the hoop marks. Lay the fabric over the pattern and trace the leaves.
2. Lay the fleece on the table and center the fabric over the fleece. Pin the 2 together, placing pins every 4". Apply resist to the leaf and flower edges.
3. Mix green with varying amounts of water to create a variety of shades. For large leaves, start at the center with a ½" flat brush and lightly paint with water first. This will prevent brush strokes from showing. Paint with green immediately. Finish painting the other leaves in shades of green.

Painting the Background

1. Apply resist around all the painted edges. Mix turquoise with 3 parts water. Start in the upper corner with a 1" flat brush and brush quickly, overlapping your strokes to prevent brush marks. Use smaller brushes between the flowers and leaves.
2. Let dry overnight. Press on the wrong side for 2 to 3 minutes, moving the iron as you heat set the paint. Rinse in cool water for 20 minutes to dissolve the resist. Lay out on a towel and dry flat.
3. If resist covered the stamen, paint over it with opaque pearl. Allow to dry and heat set as before.

Painting the Border Fabric

Following the general directions for "Scrunch, Dip, and Dye" on page 23, dye the border fabric. I used yellow and turquoise Colorhue dyes.

Hummingbird and hibiscus with leaves

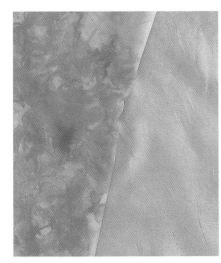

Border fabric before and after dyeing

Finished painting of Hummingbird and Hibiscus panel on silk

Tip

To create a more abstract background, I painted leaves randomly with pernod yellow, then painted the background turquoise. I dried the fabric, then drew more leaves with resist. I painted pernod yellow over the new leaf shapes, turning the turquoise to emerald green.

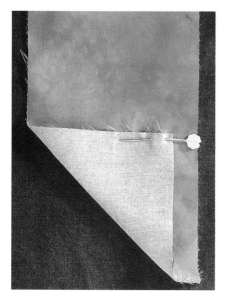

Step 2 of "Making the Pillow"

Making the Pillow

1. Cut four 3½"-wide strips across the width of the border fabric. From the strips, cut two 14"-long pieces and two 20"-long pieces.

2. Following the manufacturer's directions, apply fusible interfacing to the wrong sides of the pillow front, back, and border pieces. This stabilizes the silk and prevents it from slipping when sewing.

3. Pin a 14"-long border strip to the upper edge of the pillow top, right sides together; stitch with a ½" seam. Repeat along the bottom edge. Press the seams toward the border.

4. Pin a 20"-long border strip to the side edge of the pillow top, right sides together; stitch with a ½" seam. Repeat on the remaining side. Press the seam allowances toward the border.

5. Piece the pillow back as for the pillow front. Pin the pillow back to the pillow front, right sides together. Stitch ½" from the raw edges on 3 sides, leaving the fourth side open.

6. Press ½" seam allowances on the open side. Insert the pillow form; slipstitch the opening closed.

7. Fold the corner of the pillow to the corner of the center square on the front; pin. Sew a decorative button through all layers of the fabric. Repeat at the remaining corners.

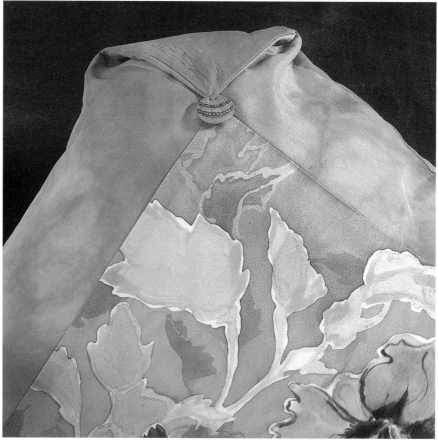

Step 7 of "Making the Pillow"

Connect to upper-right quadrant on page 82.

Connect to lower-left quadrant on page 80.

Hibiscus and Hummingbird Pillow
Upper-Left Quadrant

Connect to lower-right quadrant on page 81.

Connect to upper-left quadrant on page 79.

Hibiscus and Hummingbird Pillow
Lower-Left Quadrant

Connect to upper-right quadrant on page 82.

Connect to lower-left quadrant on page 80.

Hibiscus and Hummingbird Pillow
Lower-Right Quadrant

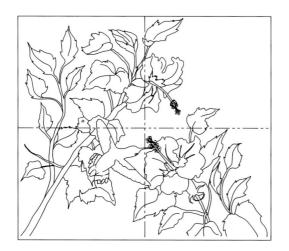

Connect to lower-right quadrant on page 82.

Connect to upper-left quadrant on page 79.

Hibiscus and Hummingbird Pillow
Upper-Right Quadrant

COLUMBINE AND HUMMINGBIRD WALL HANGING

This wall hanging features an intricate hummingbird. The detail in the bird was achieved by using a photo transfer.

NOTE: Refer to the general directions for "Faux Batik: Painting with Resist" on page 34 for information about using resist and to "Sponge Painting" on page 25 for details and tips.

Materials

14" x 17" piece of white silk or cotton for center panel
¾ yd. fabric for backing and sleeve
¼ yd. fabric for border
¼ yd. fabric for binding
20" x 23" piece of smooth fleece or batting, such as Warm & Natural or Pellon Thermolam
Photo transfer materials as listed on page 36
Setacolor transparent paints: yellow, fuchsia, purple, green, blue, pearl white, pink
Silkpaint resist in applicator with 7-mm tip
Brushes: liner brush, ½" flat brush, 2" foam brush
Sea sponge
Invisible thread or machine-embroidery thread
Bobbin thread, preferably cotton
Sewing machine with darning or free-motion embroidery foot
Machine-embroidery needle, size 75 Sharp
Gridded cutting mat
Stencil tape
1" safety pins
Air-soluble or water-soluble marking pen
Tracing paper
Press cloth
Iron and ironing board
Hair dryer (optional)
Small containers for mixing paint
Plastic drop cloth
Masking tape
Needle and thread
Scrap fabrics

Directions for Painting

1. Trace or photocopy the pattern on pages 87–90 onto paper; tape sections together as necessary.
2. With an air-soluble marker, trace the position of the hummingbird onto the fabric for the center panel. Transfer the hummingbird image (page 86) directly onto the panel as described in "Photo Transfer" on page 35. Use the pattern as a guide for placement.
3. Tape the paper pattern to a flat surface. Lay the fabric on top and tape the corners and center of each side to prevent movement. Trace the columbine flowers and leaves with an air-soluble marking pen. Remove the pattern.
4. Tape plastic to table. Lay the fabric on the center of the 20" x 23" piece of fleece. Pin the fabric to the fleece close to the fabric edge on all sides.

5. Outline the flowers and leaves with resist. Make sure the resist lines have no open areas where the paint will seep out.

6. Using small containers, dilute the Setacolor paints with equal amounts of water. Use yellow, fuchsia, and purple for the flowers and green for the leaves. Start by painting in the center of each flower or leaf, letting the paint spread up to the resist. Use the liner brush for the narrow areas of the flowers and the ½" brush for the wider areas.

7. Paint the background behind the flowers with a light wash of Setacolor green. Mix 4 parts water to 1 part paint for the wash. Paint the background with the 2" foam brush. While the fabric is damp, sponge on undiluted purple, yellow, and green paints with the sea sponge.

8. Mix and paint the sky behind the bird with a blue wash as in step 7. Mix pearl white for the clouds: 2 parts water to 1 part paint. Paint pearl white onto the fabric in cloud shapes. Let the paint dry or dry it with a hair dryer.

9. Mix a pink wash as in step 7 and paint unevenly over the pearl white.

10. Let the fabric dry overnight.

11. Unpin the fabric from the fleece. Since the fleece will be used in the quilting steps, rinse it in cool water; let dry and press.

12. Cover the fabric with a press cloth and press as on page 12 to heat set the Setacolor paint.

Directions for Assembly

NOTE: See page 50 for "Machine Embroidery."

1. Cut the backing fabric the same size as your fleece. Press and lay the backing on top of a smooth surface, wrong side up. Lay the fleece on top. Center the painted fabric over the fleece.

2. Starting at the center, pin through all layers with the safety pins. Do not pin on the photo-transferred hummingbird. Pin about every 4".

3. The fabric can be quilted with invisible thread, or if you prefer to add color, machine-embroidery thread. Loosen the sewing-machine top tension one whole number. Keep the feed dogs up. Insert the machine-embroidery needle and attach the darning foot.

4. Lower the presser foot and bring up the bobbin thread. Set the machine for straight stitching. To practice stitching, layer scrap fabrics and fleece to make a sandwich with the fleece in the middle. The free-motion foot overrides the stitch length, so the faster you move, the longer the stitch. Practice until your stitching is even. To knot the thread, take a few stitches in place.

5. Remember to bring up your bobbin thread when starting. Outline the shapes of the leaves, flowers, and sky with free-motion stitching. Add color and detail to the bird with a variety of embroidery threads and straight stitches in a small scallop pattern to imitate feathers

6. Lay the quilt over a gridded cutting mat. Using an air-soluble or water-soluble marking pen, draw a 13¼" x 16¼" rectangle, centering the painted design in the rectangle. These lines are placement lines for the border strips.

7. Cut strips of fabric 2⅝" wide for the borders. Cut one 16¼" length from the strip for the left border, one 15⅜" strip for the bottom border, one 18⅜" strip for the right border, and one 17¾" strip for the top border.

> Tip
>
> I prefer to use YLI cotton basting thread in the bobbin. If that is not readily available, a lightweight cotton embroidery thread is best. This allows the top thread to be the dominant thread, with a minimal amount of the bobbin thread showing.

Step 5 of "Directions for Assembly"

8. Pin the left border to the left side, placing it on the marked line. Stitch ¼" from the line; press. Repeat for the other 3 sides, stitching, in order, the bottom, right, and top border in place.

9. Lay the quilt over a gridded mat. Extend the ruler ¼" past the border and trim the fleece and backing.

10. Cut a 6" x 17" rectangle for the fabric sleeve. Turn up ¼" twice on each short end; stitch close to the first fold. Fold the rectangle wrong sides together, matching the raw edges. Pin the raw edges to the upper edge of the wall hanging on the back side. Baste ¼" from the upper edges. Hand stitch the lower edge of the fabric sleeve to the quilt back.

11. Cut a 1¾"-wide binding strip on the straight of grain for each side of the wall hanging. Press one side of each strip under ¼". Pin the unpressed side of one strip along the edge of the border fabric, right sides together. Stitch ¼" from the edge. Fold the binding over the fleece and around to the back of the quilt. Pin the binding so that the binding in the back is approximately ⅛" wider than the binding in the front; avoid catching the fabric sleeve in the binding. Using thread the same color as the binding, stitch "in the ditch" (right next to the seam line, away from the seam allowance) of the binding seam. Repeat on the remaining sides, concealing the raw edges of the binding at the corners.

Hummingbird, photographed by Beth Kingsley Hawkins

In this view, the humming-bird has been cut out and rotated for use on the wall hanging.

Connect to upper-right quadrant on page 88.

Connect to lower-left quadrant on page 89.

Columbine and Hummingbird Wall Hanging
Upper-Left Quadrant

Connect to upper-left quadrant on page 87.

Connect to lower-right quadrant on page 90.

Columbine and Hummingbird Wall Hanging
Upper-Right Quadrant

Connect to upper-left quadrant on page 87.

Connect to lower-right quadrant on page 90.

Columbine and Hummingbird Wall Hanging
Lower-Left Quadrant

Connect to upper-right quadrant on page 88.

Connect to lower-left quadrant on page 89.

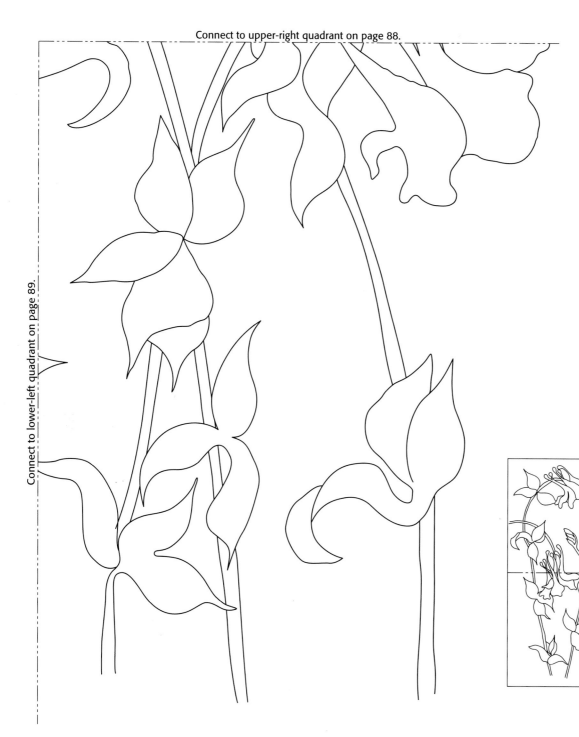

Columbine and Hummingbird Wall Hanging
Lower-Right Quadrant

PAINTED TABLE LINENS

Use these painted linens as a fun way to dress up your table, or create them for a gift. Any fabric can be used. I prefer to use washable fabrics, as someone always spills something during a celebration! The sample here is made from ready-made napkins and place mats that are 100% polyester. Always prewash and dry the fabrics before painting to remove sizing and allow for shrinkage. The smoother the texture of the fabric, the more even and solid the leaf print will be. If the fabric has raised threads or slubs, the leaf print will be abstracted. The fabric I used has raised threads, making the print uneven.

Linens are embellished with leaf prints and stenciled flowers and berries.

Materials

Ready-made table linens
Real leaves on twigs
Gold and white Lumiere paint
Red fabric paint
Fine-line paintbrush and two ¼" flat paintbrushes
Brown fine-tip fabric marker
Ready-made stencil of a flower
Circle templates
Tissue paper
Scrap paper
Paper towels
Iron and ironing board
Hair dryer (optional)
Plastic drop cloth
Masking tape

Directions

1. Choose leaves that have pronounced veins. Cut several small twigs, about 4" to 5" long. Trim off the lower leaves, leaving 3 leaves at the top. The twig works like a handle.

2. Protect the table with plastic. Stir the gold Lumiere paint. Using a ¼" brush, paint the back of the leaves and that side of the twig.

3. Lay the leaves on top of the scrap paper, lay the tissue paper over the leaves, and press. Remove the tissue. Remove the leaves. Variations can be achieved by varying the sizes of the leaves and lapping some leaf prints on top of one another. After practicing a few times, print the leaves on the corners of a place mat or napkin.

4. Clean the brush and replace the lid on the gold paint. Using a circle template and the other ¼" brush, paint red berries out from the leaves. Do a few on paper first. Be careful not to lay the template over previously painted areas that are still wet. A hair dryer can speed up the drying process if you are placing several berries next to one another.

5. Stir the white Lumiere paint. Lay the flower stencil over the paper and practice painting the flower. Do not push the paint under the stencil, or the design will smear. Using a ¼" brush, paint the flower away from the leaves.

6. Put away the white paint, clean the brush, and get out the gold Lumiere paint and liner brush. Stir the paint; then dip the tip of a liner brush in the paint. Paint lines below the berries and flowers, creating stems that go back to the branch. Gold lines can also be added to the leaves to provide definition and detail.

7. To add detail to the edge of the leaves, outline *parts* of the leaves with the brown marker. (A softer and more interesting look is achieved by partial outlining.) Again, practice by drawing around some of the gold leaves you printed on paper.

8. Allow the paints to dry for 24 hours. To set the paints, cover with a paper towel and press. I press for several seconds without moving the iron; then I lift the paper towel to see if any paint comes off on the paper. If there is paint, lay a clean paper towel over the paint and again press without moving the iron. If you move the iron and the paint is not completely dry, the paint will smear. Once the paper towel is clean, press another 20 seconds over the area, moving slowly.

Sources and Suppliers

Artex Manufacturing Company
5894 Blackwelder Street
Culver City, CA 90232-7304
Phone: 310-204-6900
Web site: www.novacolorpaint.com
Novacolor paint only

Art Quilt Magazine
PO Box 630927
Houston, TX 77263
Phone: 1-800-399-3532
Fax: 713-975-6072
E-mail: artquiltmg@aol.com
Features the latest in contemporary fiber art. The company also sells a full range of books.

Bear-Air
15 Tech Circle
Natick, MA 01760-1026
Phone: 1-800-BEARAIR
Airbrushes, airbrush paint, videos

Dharma Trading Co.
PO Box 150916
San Rafael, CA 94915
Phone: 1-800-542-5227
Web site: www.dharmatrading.com
Full line of paints, resists, brushes, and more

Ginny Eckley
2423 Kings Forest Drive
Kingwood, TX 77339
Phone: 281-358-2951
E-mail: arthread@vonl.com
Web site: www.fabricpainting.com
Workshops and commissions

Pro Chemical & Dye, Inc.
PO Box 14
Somerset, MA 02726
Phone: 508-676-3838
Fabric frames, paint, dyes, markers, books, workshops, and more

ReVisions
Diane Ericson
Box 7404
Carmel, CA 93921
Web site: www.revisions-ericson.com
Stencils, wearable-art patterns, and workshops

Rupert, Gibbon & Spider
PO Box 425
Healdsburg, CA 95448
Phone: 1-800-442-0455
Full line of fabrics and hemmed scarves for painting and dyeing

Thai Silks
252 State Street
Los Altos, CA 94022
Phone: 1-800-722-SILK
(In CA): 1-800-221-SILK
Silk fabrics

Things Japanese
9805 NE 116th, Suite 7160
Kirkland, WA 98034-4248
Phone: 425-821-3554
E-mail: thingsjapanese@seanet.com
Colorhue dye, Lumiere and Neopaque fabric paints, silk ribbon and thread, videos and books

Joan Toomey
13626 Dornock Court
Herndon, VA 20171
Phone: 703-689-0951
E-mail: RibbonsAnd@aol.com
Workshops

About the Author

The mosaic of Ginny Eckley's life began with her family. Her mother taught her patience and gratefulness. Her father instilled discipline and the sense of reality needed to make it in the world. As a college student, Ginny realized she needed art classes when her dad couldn't identify the Madonna and Child in the batik painting she presented at Christmas. She eventually earned a degree in fine art.

After college, Ginny found satisfaction in the "great exchange" of teaching: students and teacher sharing ideas, techniques, and laughter while creating together. Since the publication of her first book, *Quilted Sea Tapestries*, she has taken her fiber-art classes across the United States and Japan. She believes the urge to create is fundamental and art and learning should be fun.

Ginny's love of nature is as deep as her love of art. These passions are the basis of her work. In her art, she combines her skills with her inner thoughts and her hope that others will appreciate her creations.

Martingale & Company
Toll-free: 1-800-426-3126

International: 1-425-483-3313
24-Hour Fax: 1-425-486-7596

PO Box 118, Bothell, WA 98041-0118 USA

Web site: www.patchwork.com
E-mail: info@martingale-pub.com

Books from

These books are available through your local quilt, fabric, craft-supply, or art-supply store. For more information, contact us for a free full-color catalog. You can also find our full catalog of books online at www.patchwork.com.

Appliqué

Appliqué for Baby
Appliqué in Bloom
Baltimore Bouquets
Basic Quiltmaking Techniques for Hand Appliqué
Basic Quiltmaking Techniques for Machine Appliqué
Coxcomb Quilt
The Easy Art of Appliqué
Folk Art Animals
Fun with Sunbonnet Sue
Garden Appliqué
The Nursery Rhyme Quilt
Red and Green: An Appliqué Tradition
Rose Sampler Supreme
Stars in the Garden
Sunbonnet Sue All Through the Year

Beginning Quiltmaking

Basic Quiltmaking Techniques for Borders & Bindings
Basic Quiltmaking Techniques for Curved Piecing
Basic Quiltmaking Techniques for Divided Circles
Basic Quiltmaking Techniques for Eight-Pointed Stars
Basic Quiltmaking Techniques for Hand Appliqué
Basic Quiltmaking Techniques for Machine Appliqué
Basic Quiltmaking Techniques for Strip Piecing
The Quilter's Handbook
Your First Quilt Book (or it should be!)

Crafts

15 Beads
Fabric Mosaics
Folded Fabric Fun
Making Memories

Cross-Stitch & Embroidery

Hand-Stitched Samplers from I Done My Best
Kitties to Stitch and Quilt: 15 Redwork Designs
Miniature Baltimore Album Quilts
A Silk-Ribbon Album

Designing Quilts

Color: The Quilter's Guide
Design Essentials: The Quilter's Guide
Design Your Own Quilts
Designing Quilts: The Value of Value
The Nature of Design
QuiltSkills
Sensational Settings
Surprising Designs from Traditional Quilt Blocks
Whimsies & Whynots

Holiday

Christmas Ribbonry
Easy Seasonal Wall Quilts
Favorite Christmas Quilts from That Patchwork Place
Holiday Happenings
Quilted for Christmas
Quilted for Christmas, Book IV
Special-Occasion Table Runners
Welcome to the North Pole

Home Decorating

The Home Decorator's Stamping Book
Make Room for Quilts
Special-Occasion Table Runners
Stitch & Stencil
Welcome Home: Debbie Mumm
Welcome Home: Kaffe Fassett

Knitting

Simply Beautiful Sweaters
Two Sticks and a String

Paper Arts

The Art of Handmade Paper and Collage
Grow Your Own Paper
Stamp with Style

Paper Piecing

Classic Quilts with Precise Foundation Piecing
Easy Machine Paper Piecing
Easy Mix & Match Machine Paper Piecing
Easy Paper-Pieced Keepsake Quilts
Easy Paper-Pieced Miniatures
Easy Reversible Vests
Go Wild with Quilts
Go Wild with Quilts—Again!
It's Raining Cats & Dogs
Mariner's Medallion
Needles and Notions
Paper-Pieced Curves
Paper Piecing the Seasons
A Quilter's Ark
Sewing on the Line
Show Me How to Paper Piece

Quilting & Finishing Techniques

The Border Workbook
Borders by Design
A Fine Finish
Happy Endings
Interlacing Borders
Lap Quilting Lives!
Loving Stitches
Machine Quilting Made Easy
Quilt It!
Quilting Design Sourcebook
Quilting Makes the Quilt
The Ultimate Book of Quilt Labels

Ribbonry

Christmas Ribbonry
A Passion for Ribbonry
Wedding Ribbonry

Rotary Cutting & Speed Piecing

101 Fabulous Rotary-Cut Quilts
365 Quilt Blocks a Year Perpetual Calendar
All-Star Sampler
Around the Block with Judy Hopkins
Basic Quiltmaking Techniques for Strip Piecing
Beyond Log Cabin
Block by Block
Easy Stash Quilts
Fat Quarter Quilts
The Joy of Quilting
A New Twist on Triangles
A Perfect Match
Quilters on the Go
ScrapMania
Shortcuts
Simply Scrappy Quilts
Spectacular Scraps
Square Dance
Stripples Strikes Again!
Strips That Sizzle
Surprising Designs from Traditional Quilt Blocks

Traditional Quilts with Painless Borders
Time-Crunch Quilts
Two-Color Quilts

Small & Miniature Quilts

Bunnies by the Bay Meets Little Quilts
Celebrate! With Little Quilts
Easy Paper-Pieced Miniatures
Fun with Miniature Log Cabin Blocks
Little Quilts all Through the House
Living with Little Quilts
Miniature Baltimore Album Quilts
A Silk-Ribbon Album
Small Quilts Made Easy
Small Wonders

Surface Design

Complex Cloth
Creative Marbling on Fabric
Dyes & Paints
Fantasy Fabrics
Hand-Dyed Fabric Made Easy
Jazz It Up
Machine Quilting with Decorative Threads
New Directions in Chenille
Thread Magic
Threadplay with Libby Lehman

Topics in Quiltmaking

Bargello Quilts
The Cat's Meow
Even More Quilts for Baby
Everyday Angels in Extraordinary Quilts
Fabric Collage Quilts
Fast-and-Fun Stenciled Quilts
Folk Art Quilts
It's Raining Cats & Dogs
Kitties to Stitch and Quilt: 15 Redwork Designs
Life in the Country with Country Threads
Machine-Stitched Cathedral Windows
More Quilts for Baby
A New Slant on Bargello Quilts
Patchwork Pantry
Pink Ribbon Quilts
Quilted Landscapes
The Quilted Nursery
Quilting Your Memories
Quilts for Baby
Quilts from Aunt Amy
Whimsies & Whynots

Watercolor Quilts

More Strip-Pieced Watercolor Magic
Quick Watercolor Quilts
Strip-Pieced Watercolor Magic
Watercolor Impressions
Watercolor Quilts

Wearables

Easy Reversible Vests
Just Like Mommy
New Directions in Chenille
Quick-Sew Fleece
Variations in Chenille